Lamphege
Falles

Cochecow

Back River

Fresh Creeke

Dongreys
Edges

Dover
Iohnsons P.

Sturgen Creeke

Kettry

Moody Poine

Long
Reach

Bank Marsh

Bank

Sprus Creeke

Braberd Harbour

Agamenticus River

York Town

Great Iland

Great House

Champernones Iland

A Seale of 3 Miles.

**THE UNIVERSITY COLLEGE OF
RIPON AND YORK ST. JOHN
YORK CAMPUS**

Please return this book by the date stamped below
- if recalled, the loan is reduced to 10 days

Fines are payable for late return

Atlas of the World
in the
Age of Discovery
1453-1763

Longman

Editorial

Above: An Inca religious festival. The Spanish conquered the Inca empire in South America in the mid-16th century. Right: A Portuguese caravel, late 15th century. Below: Robert Clive of the East India Company is granted permission to collect revenues by the Mughal emperor. Previous page: An Arab astrolabe (navigational instrument) of the early 18th century. Endpapers: A detail from a 17th-century map of New England.

Author
W. D. Townson

Editor
Frances M. Clapham

Assistant Editor
Fay Franklin

LONGMAN GROUP LIMITED
Longman House
Burnt Mill, Harlow, Essex

First published 1981

Designed and produced by Grisewood & Dempsey Ltd
Elsley Court, 20–22 Great Titchfield Street,
London W.1.

© Grisewood & Dempsey Ltd, 1981

Printed and bound by Vallardi Industrie Grafiche, Milan,
Italy

BRITISH LIBRARY CATALOGUING IN PUBLICATION DATA

Townson, William Duncan
Illustrated atlas of the world in the age of discovery.
1. Geography, Historical—Maps—Juvenile literature
I. Title
911   G1035

ISBN 0–582–39117–2

Contents

Above: The Spanish-built cathedral at Quito, Ecuador.

Right: An early map of the Strait of Magellan.
Below: The battle of Panipat which gave Babur control of northern India.

In 1450 the different parts of the world had little contact with one another. Some people, like the Australian Aborigines, had had no contact with others for 50,000 years. The people of North and South America were almost as cut off from the rest of the world, since the existence of the continent was not known to people outside it. Africa south of the Sahara had been largely isolated for 6000 years, since the Sahara became so dry that it was difficult to cross.

Only in Europe and Asia was there much contact between different areas and even this was confined to trade in a few articles. Textiles, pearls, gems and spices had for centuries been imported into Europe from the Far East but little was known about the lands they came from. Not till the 13th century, when missionaries and merchants such as John of Plano Carpini and Marco Polo visited Central Asia and China, did Europeans know much about Asia.

The geographical knowledge of Europeans had not changed much since the time of the Roman empire. Then the most important geographer was the Egyptian Ptolemy, who lived in Alexandria in the 2nd century AD. His *Geography* was lost for much of the Middle Ages, but was re-discovered and published in 1406. It was widely read after that, though it contained several important errors, such as indicating that there was no way round Africa, which were to hinder exploration.

All this was changed by the voyages of discovery. By 1780 the shape of all the continents was accurately known. Only the

Widening Horizons

In 1450 Europe was only one of many great civilizations, including those of China, Japan, Hindu India, the Aztecs and Incas in America, and Islam which was beginning a great movement of expansion under the Ottoman Turks. Europe was by no means the most important, civilized or wealthy of these. Yet by 1750 the situation had changed. European states had gained control of the ocean routes, organized world-wide trade and conquered vast territories in America, India and Siberia. The period from 1450 to 1750 stands halfway between the isolation of earlier centuries, and the 'one world' of the 19th and 20th centuries, when what happened in one part of the world could have important results elsewhere.

This Flemish picture was painted in the early 1600s and shows the interior of an art gallery. On the table are a globe, maps and navigational instruments including an astrolabe and a compass. These show the immense interest in exploration and discovery which people had at that time.

Knowledge of these discoveries was spread by one of the most important advances since the invention of writing: printing. Until then books were slowly copied out by hand. They were scarce and expensive and most people, even the wealthiest, could not read. The first person in Europe to use movable metal type and an oil-based ink was Johannes Gutenberg, a diamond polisher in Mainz in Germany. The 'Gutenberg Bible', which he produced in 1455, was the first European printed book. By 1500 other printers all over Europe had followed his lead and about 35,000 editions of printed books had been published – between 15 and 20 million copies, which is probably more than the total number of manuscripts copied by hand in the previous thousand years. Books were now much cheaper and easily available. More people learned to read and write than ever before and information spread quickly.

interiors of areas such as Africa south of the Sahara and Australia were unexplored.

Europeans Grow Rich

Until Columbus found America in 1492 European society had been changing very slowly. Apart from the farm land gained by clearing forest and draining marshes, the amount of land available to European farmers had remained almost unaltered.

All this changed with the discovery of the New World. American bullion, and the profitable trade carried on by the Portuguese, Dutch, English and French with India, the Spice Islands (now Indonesia) and the Far East, brought unheard of riches to Europe. The gold and silver which Drake brought back in the *Golden Hind* after his plundering expedition to Spanish America provided the money for two English trading companies, the East India Company and the Levant Company. The profits of these companies were invested, at the end of the 17th and in the 18th century, in English industries: cotton in Lancashire, iron in Birmingham and the potteries of Staffordshire. Here are the origins of the Industrial Revolution, which put Europe ahead of the world in the 19th century.

If such wealth had been spent on luxuries, jewels, vast houses and a great number of servants, in the way that Indian princes used their enormous wealth, there would have been no Industrial Revolution. What was needed to enable Europe to move from an agricultural to an industrial society was a group of people ready to seize the new opportunities and invest in industry. It was formed by merchants, bankers and businessmen. Why did such a group rise in Europe and not elsewhere? Trade was as great in India and China as it was in Europe. However, merchants in these countries were not highly regarded.

China and Japan Withdraw

Just as these pushing and confident Europeans were expanding overseas, they received an unexpected benefit. The Chinese and the Japanese withdrew of their own will from the seas. The voyages of Cheng Ho between 1405 and 1433 had shown what the Chinese were capable of doing. He had sailed round Malaya to India and then on to the Gulf in seven voyages. His first fleet consisted of 62 large ships and 28,000 men. However, a decree from the Chinese emperor ended these voyages. The Tokugawa ruler of Japan also cut his country off from the outside world in 1635, when Japanese were forbidden to travel abroad. If the Chinese and the Japanese had resisted the Europeans, instead of ignoring them, the history of the world might well have been different.

Europe's Impact on the World

In spite of the vast empire they conquered, the impact of Europeans on most parts of

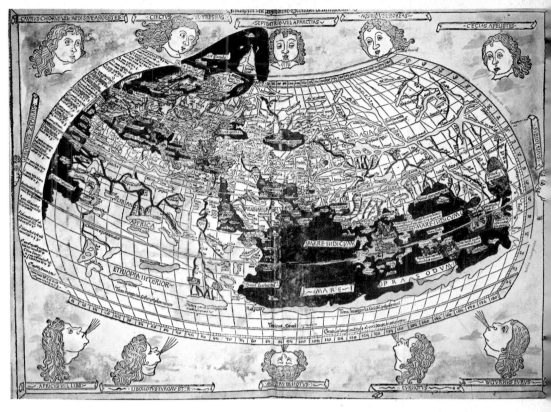

the world between 1450 and 1750 was not very great. China and Japan continued in their own way, unaffected by what Europeans were doing. In Africa and India European influence was limited generally to scattered areas on or near the coast. Only in America and some of the Spice Islands did Europeans overthrow an existing way of life and deeply affect the inhabitants. Not until the new scientific discoveries and their application in the Industrial Revolution in the 19th century did Europe profoundly affect the rest of the world.

In Europe too the number of people directly affected by the voyages of discovery was small. Life went on as it had been going on for centuries. Most people lived their lives in the village in which they were born and rarely, if ever, moved beyond the nearest market town. The slow rhythm of the seasons and the need to get in the harvest decided their pattern of work and leisure.

The map above dates from 1486 and is based on the world of Ptolemy, who lived in the 2nd century AD. America had not yet been discovered, and no one knew how far south Africa stretched. Below is a map of the world printed in 1570, less than 100 years later. By then Dias had sailed round Africa, da Gama had gone on to India, and Columbus, Vespucci and Magellan had explored the coasts of America. In the south is shown the huge block of 'Terra Australis nondum Cognita', the unknown land to the south; not until Cook's voyages of the 1770s was this shown not to exist.

Ships, Navigation and Guns

Before explorers could find an all-sea route to the Spice Islands (Indonesia), they needed ships which were strong enough to brave the stormy seas of the Atlantic and to battle against the wind down the coast of Africa. The first ships capable of doing this were developed by the Portuguese and the Spaniards, and so it was they, rather than the Arabs or Chinese, who discovered America and sailed round the world.

In 1450 there were no ships which were capable of long journeys in open seas. The Arabs were masters of the Indian Ocean but their ships, called dhows, were difficult to hold on course, particularly as they were steered by an oar. The planks were held together by wooden pegs and coconut fibre rope, which were weaker on the open sea than the nailed planks of the European ships. Chinese junks sailed long distances, but they had to have the wind behind them and were often driven helplessly off course by storms. The long, narrow oared galleys of the Mediterranean could not stand up to the Atlantic breakers, while the cargo-carrying cog of northern Europe was heavy and slow. It had a square sail, which prevented it sailing near the wind.

In the middle of the 15th century the Portuguese developed a new type of ship, the *caravel*. It was small and light, with a triangular lateen sail, so that it could sail close to the wind. By the end of the century another and larger ship, the *nao*, had been designed. It had high castles (built-up ends), large holds and both square and lateen sails. By 1500 all European ships had this combination of sails, making them more manoeuvrable than any other type of ship in the world.

After this ships became bigger but their design was basically unchanged until the steam ship. The captain of a 19th-century clipper would have felt at home in Columbus's ships, though he would have found them small and cramped.

Navigation

When they were out of sight of land, sailors needed to work out their position at sea. The compass, which had been used at sea since about 1250, told them in which direction they were going, as the needle always pointed north. It was much more difficult to work out how far they had travelled in any direction.

Latitude (movement north or south) could be measured by finding the angle of the Sun above the horizon at noon. To do this instruments such as the astrolabe or cross staff were used. With the help of tables, which gave the position of the Sun at different latitudes for each day of the year, a sea captain could work out how far north or south of the Equator he was, to within about 48 kilometres (30 miles). Accurate tables were needed for this. These were provided by Prince

Top: A caravel of the late 1400s, the sort of ship in which the Portuguese sailed southwards to explore the coasts of Africa.

Above: A reconstruction of the 'Santa Maria', the ship in which Christopher Columbus made his first Atlantic crossing in 1492. With him were two smaller caravels, the 'Nina' and the 'Pinta'. He sailed first to the Canary Islands, as he knew winds there blew to the west. When he left the Canaries he was very fortunate, as the winds blew steadily. Even so, after 30 days at sea the crew of the 'Santa Maria' demanded that he should turn back. He agreed to do so within a few days if land had not been sighted, but two days later a lookout on the 'Pinta' saw land. They had reached the Bahamas islands.

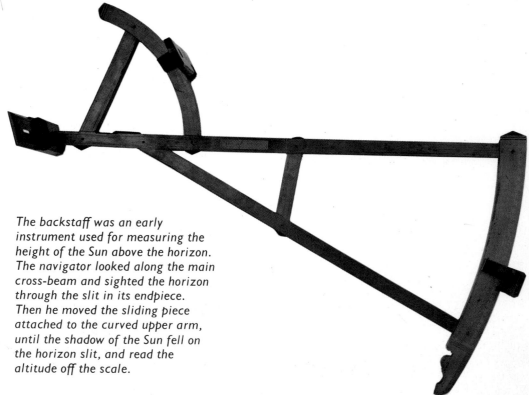

The backstaff was an early instrument used for measuring the height of the Sun above the horizon. The navigator looked along the main cross-beam and sighted the horizon through the slit in its endpiece. Then he moved the sliding piece attached to the curved upper arm, until the shadow of the Sun fell on the horizon slit, and read the altitude off the scale.

Henry 'the Navigator' of Portugal (1394–1460), whose astronomers and mathematicians worked out the necessary information for Portuguese seamen.

There was no accurate way of deciding longitude (movement east or west) until the marine chronometer was invented in 1762. In spite of this, knowledge of latitude enabled seamen to travel long distances across the open sea and yet steer a ship to a particular place. In 1497 Vasco da Gama spent 97 days out of sight of land and still steered accurately for the Cape of Good Hope.

Guns

Europeans sailing into unknown waters did not only need stout ships and aids to navigation. They also had to be able to defend themselves. In the Middle Ages warships carried soldiers, who boarded an enemy ship after it had been rammed. So naval battles then took the form of hand-to-hand fighting on deck. This continued in the Mediterranean as late as the battle of Lepanto in 1571.

In the 15th century guns were fitted to European ships, but they were only small. They could kill men but not damage ships. Between 1500 and 1520 new methods for casting guns were developed in the Netherlands and Germany which gave greater firepower. These guns could fire round stones, and later cast-iron balls, that weighed from about 2 to 27 kilograms (5 to 60 pounds) and could damage ships 275 metres (300 yards) away. The aim now was not to ram and board the enemy ship but to sink it by gunfire. This new type of warfare meant that ships had to be built more strongly with a large keel, heavy ribs and double oak planking. Soon they could carry 40 guns and could take the recoil of cannon without being damaged. Europeans had learned to build stout ships to sail the Atlantic. Ships built for less stormy seas fell apart after a few shots had been fired. No Asian country learned to redesign its ships to carry heavy guns, so the Europeans had a great advantage that enabled them to seize and keep control of the oceans of the world. From 1500 their supremacy was not successfully challenged until 1905, when the Japanese (who had learned to build western-style ships) defeated the Russian fleet at Tsushima.

The traverse board helped sailors know how far they had sailed. The helmsman inserted pegs to show how many half-hour periods the ship had sailed on any particular course. Estimated speed was shown in the four rows of holes at the foot of the board. Below: The defeat of the Spanish Armada. The English ships were faster and more manoeuvrable than the great Spanish galleons, and their guns had a longer range.

The World in 1450

In Europe, this is a time of change. The feudal system is breaking down. In the independent cities of northern Italy a new interest in learning and art is growing up; it spreads through Europe, helped by the invention of the printing press in the 1450s. Soon the western Church will be split when Protestants break away in the Reformation. In 1453 the Ottoman Turks capture Constantinople, the last stronghold of the Byzantine empire. In Portugal Prince Henry the Navigator gathers sailors, mapmakers, and ship designers; the great age of exploration is about to begin.

Western Europe The devastation caused by the Black Death of the 1340s has helped break down the feudal system; central governments are being formed. The Hundred
5 Years War between England and France ends in 1453 with the loss of almost all England's lands in France. The Italian Renaissance – an increasing interest in learning and the arts – soon spreads northwards. In Germany 7 Gutenberg invents his printing process.

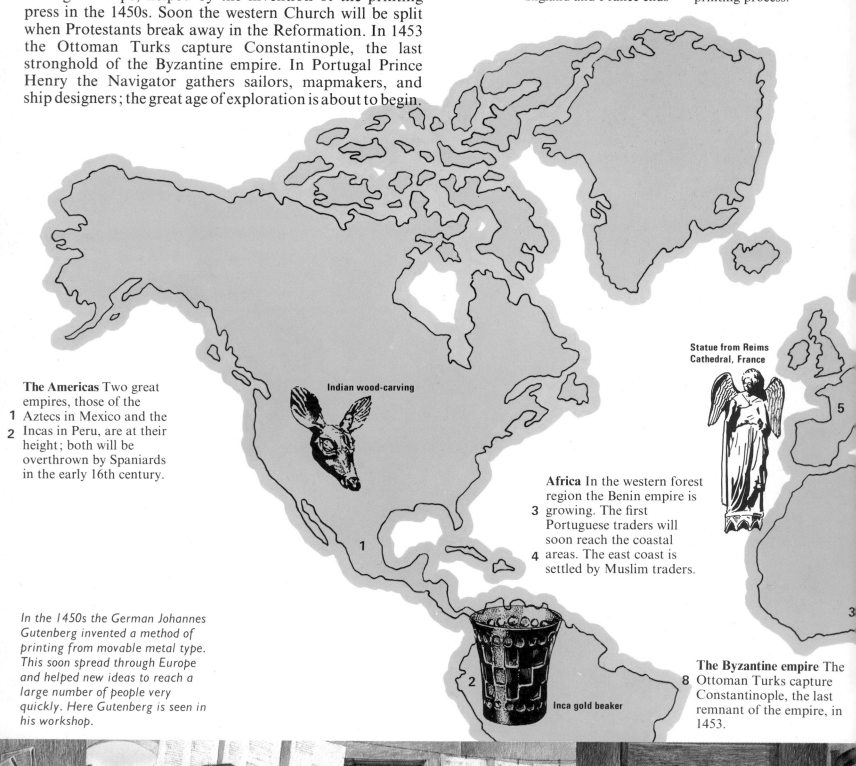

Indian wood-carving

The Americas Two great empires, those of the
1 Aztecs in Mexico and the
2 Incas in Peru, are at their height; both will be overthrown by Spaniards in the early 16th century.

Statue from Reims Cathedral, France

Africa In the western forest region the Benin empire is
3 growing. The first Portuguese traders will soon reach the coastal
4 areas. The east coast is settled by Muslim traders.

In the 1450s the German Johannes Gutenberg invented a method of printing from movable metal type. This soon spread through Europe and helped new ideas to reach a large number of people very quickly. Here Gutenberg is seen in his workshop.

Inca gold beaker

The Byzantine empire The
8 Ottoman Turks capture Constantinople, the last remnant of the empire, in 1453.

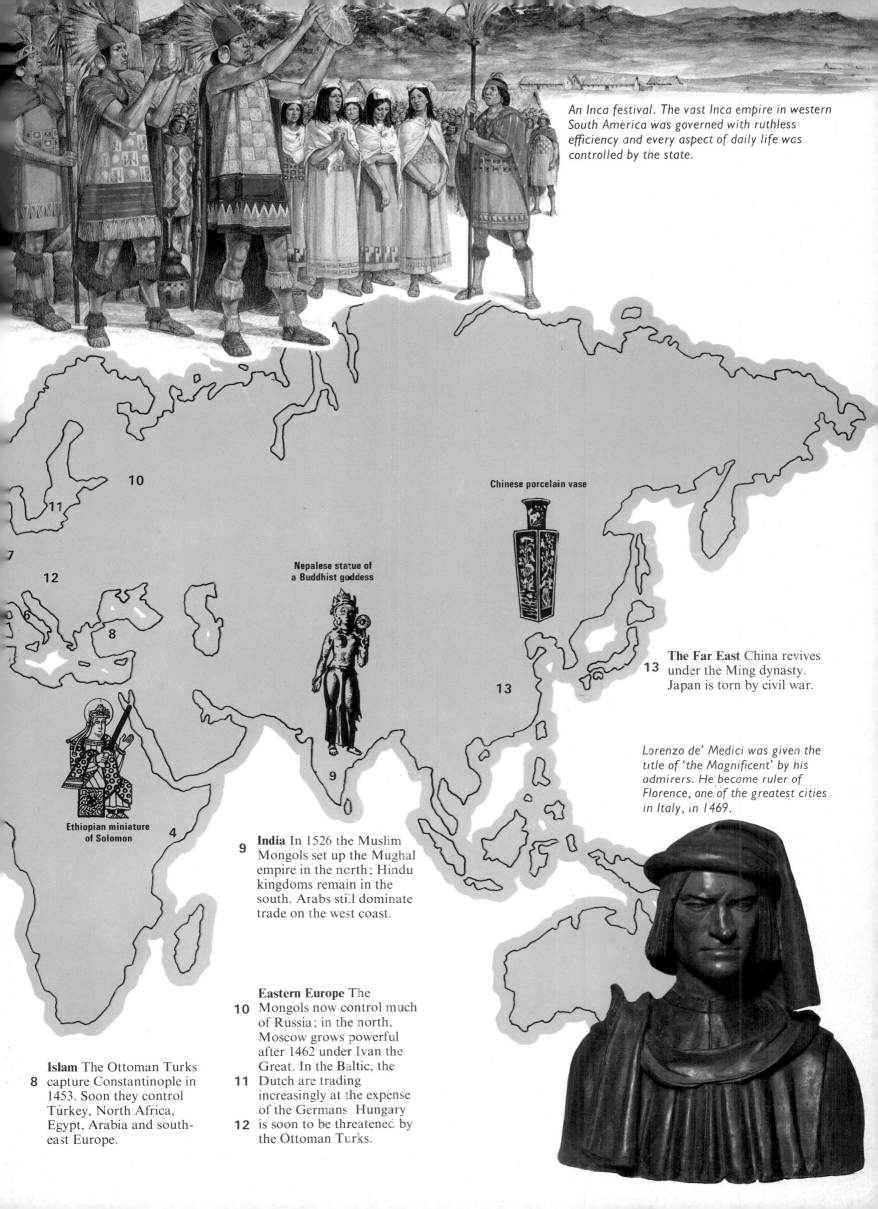

An Inca festival. The vast Inca empire in western South America was governed with ruthless efficiency and every aspect of daily life was controlled by the state.

Chinese porcelain vase

Nepalese statue of a Buddhist goddess

The Far East China revives
13 under the Ming dynasty. Japan is torn by civil war.

Lorenzo de' Medici was given the title of 'the Magnificent' by his admirers. He became ruler of Florence, one of the greatest cities in Italy, in 1469.

Ethiopian miniature of Solomon

India In 1526 the Muslim
9 Mongols set up the Mughal empire in the north; Hindu kingdoms remain in the south. Arabs still dominate trade on the west coast.

Eastern Europe The
10 Mongols now control much of Russia; in the north, Moscow grows powerful after 1462 under Ivan the Great. In the Baltic, the
11 Dutch are trading increasingly at the expense of the Germans. Hungary
12 is soon to be threatened by the Ottoman Turks.

Islam The Ottoman Turks
8 capture Constantinople in 1453. Soon they control Turkey, North Africa, Egypt, Arabia and south-east Europe.

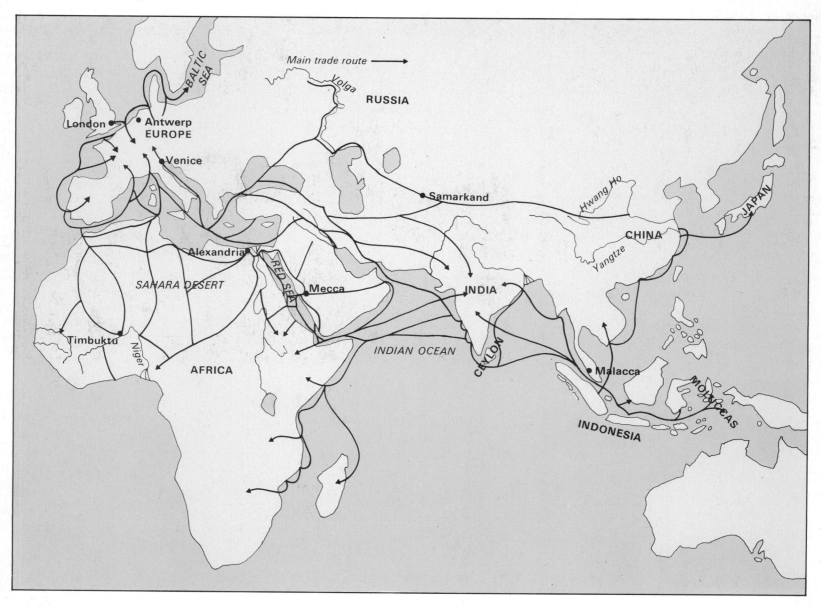

World Trade in 1450

In 1450 there was little trade between Europe and Asia. Moving goods was a slow and costly business, so only valuable luxuries could be moved great distances and still make a profit. There was much more trade within the continents of Europe and Asia than between them.

Trade Within Europe
Most of the trade carried on by the Europeans in 1450 was with other European countries, as between them they produced almost all the things they needed. Northern countries around the Baltic produced grain, fish, timber and furs. Most of this trade was controlled by the Hanseatic League, a group of German cities who had trading posts as far apart as Novgorod in Russia and London. Much of their trade, including wool and cloth from England, was brought to Bruges and Antwerp in the Netherlands. These great markets were the links between north and south Europe.

Galleys from Venice came here with goods from the warm Mediterranean

countries – wine, olives, fruit and (especially important), salt. They also brought with them goods Europeans did not produce for themselves: luxuries from the East, such as spices, silks and jewels including emeralds from India and sapphires from Ceylon (Sri Lanka).

The main routes of trade in 1450. Caravans of camels carried gold and salt across the Sahara Desert, while spices from the East were taken overland from China by the Silk Road, or by sea to the Near East. Arabs had built trading ports along the East African coast, and made frequent voyages to India.

CLOVES
Antonio Pigafetta sailed with Magellan in 1519. Here he describes the most valuable spice of all. The islands are the Moluccas.

The clove tree is tall and as thick as a man's body. The cloves grow at the ends of the twigs, ten or twenty in a cluster. When the cloves sprout they are white, when ripe, red, and when dried, black. They are gathered twice a year. Those trees grow only in the mountains, and if any of them are planted in the lowlands near the mountains they do not live. No cloves are grown in the world except in the five mountains of those five islands.

THE IMPORTANCE OF SPICES

Spices were the most valuable cargoes because they were used to preserve meat and to make it more tasty. Most cattle in Europe were killed in the autumn, as there was a shortage of winter food for them. They then had to be preserved for eating. Salt was the most common preservative. Apart from salt, all spices used as preservatives came from the East. Pepper, the most common, came mainly from India and the Spice Islands (now Indonesia) in South-East Asia. Cinnamon, the bark of a tree from Ceylon (Sri Lanka), was also valued, as was ginger from China. The rarest and most prized spices, such as cloves and nutmeg, came from a small group of islands, the Moluccas.

Trade Within Asia

The Spice Islands played the same part in Asia as the Netherlands in Europe; they were the centre of a wide trading network. Ships trading between India and China had to pass through the islands. As a result Malacca in Malaya became a great and wealthy port. There Chinese merchants met traders from India, Arabia and Persia. Indians brought cotton cloth; the Arabs and Persians brought horses, dates and carpets. They traded with the islands and with each other and so brought together the trade of South-East Asia with that of China, India and the Near East. This trade was much more valuable than the trade with Europe, which was small and of little importance to Asian countries.

The Spice Routes

In the Middle Ages much of the trade between Europe and Asia had gone overland. Caravans of merchants with pack animals made the long journey from China across the oases of Central Asia to ports on the Black Sea or Mediterranean. These routes were no longer safe after the collapse of the Mongol empire in 1340, so after that most of the goods went by sea. Chinese

junks collected spices from the islands and took them to Malacca. From there Muslim merchants carried them across the Bay of Bengal and north to ports on the west coast of India, especially Calicut. They were then taken in Arab dhows either to Ormuz at the entrance to the Gulf, or up the Red Sea. Camel caravans carried the goods overland to Alexandria in Egypt or to Damascus and other markets in Syria. Here merchants from Venice bought the spices and took them to Europe.

Europeans had to pay for the spices in gold, as there was no need for European goods either in Egypt or in the Far East. They obtained this gold from the Niger area in West Africa. It was carried across the Sahara to the Mediterranean by camel, and exchanged for European manufactured goods, especially cloth.

Italian and Arab merchants made large fortunes from the spice trade. It was said that a merchant could lose five out of six cargoes and still make a profit when the sixth was sold. Naturally other European countries wanted to take part in such profitable trade. This was one of the reasons the Portuguese and Spaniards wanted to find an all-sea route to the Spice Islands.

The port of Malacca, on the west coast of the Malay peninsula, was captured by Albuquerque in 1511. It was an early centre of the spice trade. Albuquerque's son wrote: 'This port of Malacca is very safe; there are no storms to injure it, and never was a ship lost there. It forms a point where some monsoons commence and others end, so that the inhabitants of Malacca call those of India people of the West, and the Javanese, Chinese and all others of those Islanders, people of the East, and Malacca is in the middle of all this, a sure and speedy navigation.' In 1641 it was taken by the Dutch. This picture dates from around 1660.

Below: The market at Ankara in Turkey. In the background is a caravan of camels. Such caravans of merchants with camels, donkeys, horses or mules roped together and loaded with trade goods, travelled long distances over land. Along the main trading routes were 'caravanserais', groups of buildings which provided travellers with food and lodging and gave them some protection from raiders.

Voyages of Discovery

As a result of Henry the Navigator's expeditions, many Portuguese trading stations grew up along the west coast of Africa. By the time this map was drawn in 1558 much of the coast had been charted and named.

In the 15th century Portugal was a poor country. Two-thirds of the land was too rocky or steep to be cultivated. Yet Portugal was well placed to begin the explorations of the coast of Africa. Its sailors were used to the rough waters of the Atlantic. Prince Henry 'the Navigator', son of the Portuguese king, provided the leadership.

Henry the Navigator

Henry wanted to make contact by sea with the gold-producing areas of West Africa. He was a very sincere Christian and hoped not only to seize the gold trade from the Muslims but also to convert the native people of Africa to Christianity.

Cape Bojador was the southernmost limit of the Atlantic then known. Here there were violent waves and strong currents and it was difficult to turn round and sail back north because of the strong southerly winds. In 1434 one of Henry's ships rounded Cape Bojador and did return. It was his greatest achievement. After this the Portuguese lost their fear of unknown seas and were soon moving farther south. By the time Prince Henry died in 1460, the Portuguese had reached Sierra Leone. Madeira, the Azores and the Cape Verde Islands had been colonized. As the Portuguese sailed down the coast of Africa their aims changed. Instead of gold from Africa, they sought an all-sea route to the Spice Islands round southern Africa.

In 1487 Bartolomeu Dias set off to find this route. He battled down the coast in the teeth of the south-east trade winds and was blown out to sea by violent storms. When they eased off and he reached land he found that he had come round the tip of Africa.

Vasco da Gama

Vasco da Gama left Lisbon with three ships in 1497. At the Cape Verde Islands he swung far west into the Atlantic. By doing this he avoided the opposing winds along the coast and was able to pick up the Westerlies, which would bring him to the Cape. This route has been followed ever since by sailing ships. After passing the Cape he sailed up the east coast of Africa. When he reached Mozambique he found himself in a busy trading area, which had already been accurately mapped by the Arabs. He picked up an Arab pilot, Ibn Majib, who guided his ships across the Indian Ocean to Calicut. Da Gama was the first European to reach India by sea. Here he collected a cargo of pepper, cinnamon, ginger and precious stones and set sail for Portugal. He reached Lisbon in 1499. Two-thirds of his crew had died on the way, but the sale of his cargo was worth 60 times the cost of the expedition.

Christopher Columbus

Christopher Columbus, a Genoese sailor, believed that the shortest and easiest route to the Spice Islands lay in sailing west. No one in Europe then knew that there was a vast continent in the way, though the Vikings had landed in North America in the 11th century.

With the backing of Queen Isabella of Spain, Columbus set sail in 1492. He first went to the Canary Islands, as he knew that the winds there blew to the west. He sailed for over a month before reaching the Bahamas and later Cuba.

On three more voyages Columbus discovered Jamaica, Trinidad, the northern coast of South America and Central America. Until his death in 1506, he was convinced that he had reached Asia.

CHRONOLOGY

1434	Cape Bojador rounded by the Portuguese
1487	Dias leaves Lisbon to sail round the Cape and enters the Indian Ocean (1488)
1492	Columbus discovers the Bahamas islands, and explores the north coast of Cuba and Hispaniola (to 1493)
1493	Columbus explores the south coast of Cuba, thinking it is part of mainland China
1497	Da Gama sails to India (to 1499)
1498	Columbus discovers Trinidad and the coast of South America
1500	The Portuguese Pedro Cabral sees the coast of Brazil
1502	Columbus's last voyage (to 1504). He explores the coast of Central America
1519	First voyage round the world by Magellan's expedition (to 1522)

Ferdinand Magellan

Any hope of reaching the Spice Islands by sailing west now depended on finding a passage through the new continent or on sailing round it. Explorers continued to move down the coast of South America. One of these was Amerigo Vespucci, after whom America is named. The most famous of all was Ferdinand Magellan, a Portuguese in Spanish pay, who set sail from Spain in 1519. He crossed the Atlantic to Brazil and then turned south. Eventually he reached the strait at the tip of South America that was to be named after him. It was 560 kilometres (350 miles) long and full of reefs. Ice-covered mountains rose sheer on both sides and acted as a funnel for the wind, creating violent squalls. It took Magellan 38 days to sail through the strait into an ocean that was so calm and smooth that he called it 'the peaceful [Pacific] ocean'.

Magellan sailed up the coast of Chile before turning west. It was over three months before he next reached land in the Philippines. There he was killed in a local war. But one of his ships under Sebastian del Cano managed to reach Spain in 1522 and so completed the first voyage round the world.

The difficulties Magellan had found while sailing round South America meant that the Strait of Magellan would never be used as a trade route to the East. The main trade route would long continue to be the Portuguese one round Africa and across the Indian Ocean. Yet the importance of the voyages of Spain and Portugal was immense. They had found a continent previously unknown in Europe, and they had shown that all the oceans in the world were connected and that the world was much bigger than expected.

This early map of South America shows the Strait of Magellan and fanciful pictures of the local people and animals.

HARDSHIP AT SEA

Pigafetta described the terrible conditions on board Magellan's ship when sailing across the Pacific:

We were three months and twenty days without getting any kind of fresh food. We ate biscuit, which was no longer biscuit, but powder of biscuits swarming with worms, for they had eaten the good. It stank strongly of the urine of rats. We drank yellow water that had been putrid for many days. We were even forced, so that we might not die of hunger, to eat pieces of leather with which the mainyard was covered to prevent it from wearing the ropes. These pieces of leather, constantly exposed to the water, sun and wind, were so hard that they required being soaked four or five days in the sea in order to make them supple; after this we boiled them to eat. Frequently indeed we were obliged to live on sawdust, and even rats . . . were sought after with such greed that they sold for half a ducat apiece.

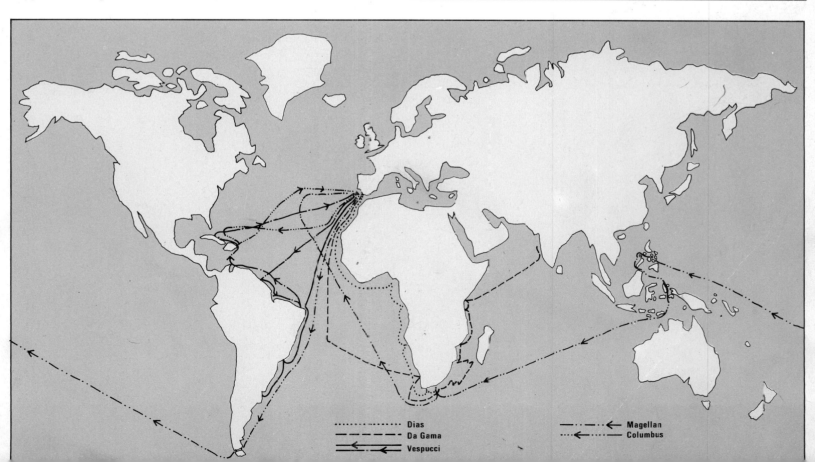

-------	Dias	------- ←	Magellan
-------	Da Gama	------ ←	Columbus
←	Vespucci		

Overseas Empires

In 1519, the same year in which Magellan left Seville on his voyage round the world (see page 17), Hernan Cortes left Cuba in the West Indies and landed on the American coast near present-day Vera Cruz. In the 30 years that followed, a few thousand Spanish adventurers (*conquistadors*) conquered the first great European overseas empire.

The Conquistadors

Although Cortes had only a small number of Spanish soldiers, he had the great advantage of having horses, gunpowder and steel weapons. The Aztecs, rulers of a great empire in Central America, had seen none of these before and were terrified by them. Cortes learned that other tribes hated the Aztecs and persuaded them to join him. In 1521 Cortes finally defeated the Aztecs and captured their capital city Tenochtitlan.

Even more remarkable than the defeat of the Aztecs was the conquest of the vast Inca empire. Soon after the conquest of Mexico rumours of the fabulous riches of the Incas in Peru reached the conquistadors. Francisco Pizarro decided to find out if they were true. He set off in 1531 from Panama in three ships with 180 men, 27 horses and 2 cannon. When he reached the port of Tumbes he heard that the Inca leader, Atahualpa, was only 565 kilometres (350 miles) away at Cajamarca. Pizarro and his men marched up the steep gorges of the Andes, breathless from lack of oxygen. At Cajamarca he captured, and later killed, Atahualpa and seized huge quantities of gold. Within 20 years the Spaniards ruled the whole Inca empire.

The success of Cortes and Pizarro inspired other conquistadors to march through large areas of both North and South America, searching for booty. They found nothing like the Aztec and Inca treasures but they conquered Central America and what is now Colombia and Venezuela. By 1550 they had followed the Amazon from Peru to its mouth. By 1600 they were familiar with the entire coast of South America, from the Gulf of California south to Tierra del Fuego and north from there to the West Indies.

Spanish helmet, sword and crossbow (16th century)

Black stone alpaca, Inca

The Royal Road of the Incas wound through the high Andes, and was used by the Inca emperor and his officials and soldiers. Ravines were crossed by rope bridges.

NEW SPAIN

Many people from Spain went to live in the new Spanish empire. These colonies were ruled by the Council of the Indies in Spain. It appointed all officials to run the new territories, especially the viceroys. One viceroy lived in Mexico City (formerly Tenochtitlan) and governed New Spain, which consisted of all Spanish lands in North America, the West Indies, Venezuela and the Philippines. The viceroy of Peru at Lima ruled the rest of Spain's possessions in South America.

Many of the laws made for the colonies show that the Spanish government tried to make sure that Indians were well-treated, but it was impossible to prevent the conquistadors from treating the Indians badly. Soon many were made slaves or were killed, while thousands died as they had no resistance to European diseases such as measles and smallpox. The population of Peru at the time of the conquest was 7 million; by 1600 it was 1,800,000.

The value of the new empire to Spain became clear in the 1540s, when silver mines were discovered in both Mexico and Peru. Potosí in Peru was the biggest source of silver in the world and was to provide Europe with most of its precious metals for the next 300 years.

The 17th-century cathedral at Quito, capital of Ecuador. The city was planned on typical Spanish lines by de Belalcazar, one of Pizarro's lieutenants, in the 1530s.

Spanish control
Portuguese control

Spanish and Portuguese lands in Central and South America. In 1494 the Tordesillas demarcation line was agreed; Portugal had the right to land east of this line, while that to the west could be claimed by Spain.

Brazil

In 1500 the Portuguese Pedro Alvares Cabral, sailing to the Indian Ocean, moved too far out into the Atlantic and reached Brazil. It was the only part of South America which became Portuguese rather than Spanish. Sugar plantations were set up near the coast. Few of the other early settlements were successful, and in the mid-16th century King John took Brazil under royal control and appointed a governor general. By 1600 Brazil had become the most important sugar-producing area in the world. When Brazil began to lose its lead in sugar production because the soil was exhausted, gold was discovered there. Much of this went to England, which supplied most of the manufactures Brazil needed.

Brazil was only one part of the Portuguese empire. More important to Portugal were its colonies in Africa and in the Spice Islands (see page 30).

A picture of Brazil in 1600. Rowing up the river, and in the stockade, are Portuguese soldiers. By this time Brazil was under the direct rule of the Portuguese king, and settlers were arriving in great numbers.

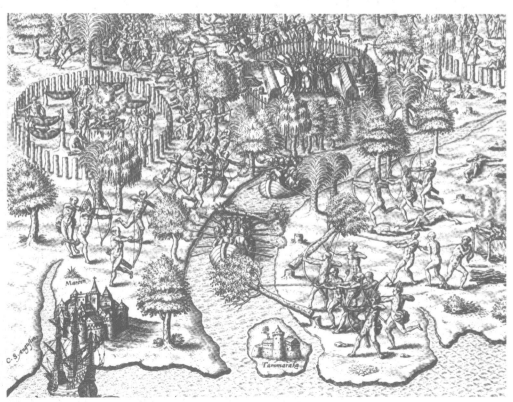

CHRONOLOGY

- **1492** Columbus reaches the Bahamas
- **1493** Spaniards begin to settle Hispaniola
- **1494** Treaty of Tordesillas signed between Spain and Portugal, giving Spain rights to all land west of line of demarcation; Portuguese retain rights to east
- **1500** Pedro Cabral claims Portugal for Brazil
- **1509** First Spanish settlement of American mainland
- **1519** Cortes begins conquest of Aztec empire
- **1523** Spanish begin to settle Guatemala
- **1532** Pizarro begins conquest of Inca empire
- **1535** Spanish establish viceroy in Mexico
- **1536** Spanish begin to settle New Granada
- **1545** Silver mines discovered at Potosi, Peru
- **1549** First governor general of Brazil brings the country under royal control
- **1564** Spanish start to send convoys of ships carrying silver back to Europe, accompanied by warships

Reformation and Counter-Reformation

In 1500 nearly everyone in Western Europe was a member of the Catholic Church but many people were discontented with it. Some rulers wanted its wealth and lands for themselves. Other people criticized the immorality and ignorance of many of the clergy, and the sale of indulgences, by which the Pope's representatives forgave people their sins in return for money.

Martin Luther

One man who showed this discontent forcefully was Martin Luther in Germany. He said that only God, not the Pope nor priests, could forgive sins. He denied that salvation from the everlasting fires of Hell depended on good deeds. Only faith in God, he said, could bring salvation. He also said that priests should be allowed to marry, as he did himself. In 1517 he publicly attacked the sale of indulgences by pinning his 95 'theses' (arguments) to the church door at Wittenberg.

In doing this Luther began a movement known as the Reformation (as it was an attempt to reform the Catholic Church), which was to lead to a split in the Church. Thanks to the invention of printing his ideas were known throughout Germany in only a few weeks. Luther's supporters set up a 'reformed' Church which became known as Protestant, a name later given to other reformed Churches as well.

In Germany many princes backed Luther in order to seize Church lands. This led to a war between the Catholic Emperor Charles V and the Protestants. Neither side won a clear victory, so in 1555 the Emperor had to allow each German prince to decide whether his state should be Catholic or Protestant. By this time Lutheranism had spread over nearly all northern Germany and Scandinavia.

John Calvin

In Switzerland appeared another great religious reformer, John Calvin. He was more severe than Luther and believed that from the moment we are born, we are destined to go to Heaven or Hell. Nothing we can do in our lives can change this. By the time Calvin died his ideas had spread to much of Switzerland, France and the Netherlands. In Scotland Calvinists led by John Knox overthrew the Catholic Mary Queen of Scots, and Calvinism became the main religion. It also spread to parts of Germany, Poland, Bohemia and Hungary.

Martin Luther, the monk who led the Protestant split from the Roman Catholic Church.

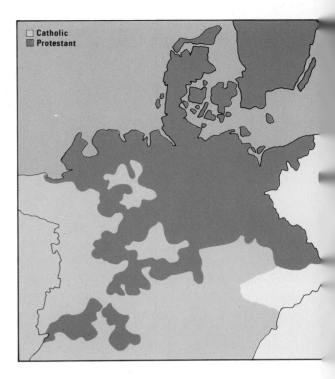

The main Protestant and Catholic areas in northern Europe in the mid-16th century. The cream-coloured region on the right was mixed. In southern Europe the Reformation had little success; Portugal, Spain, Italy and Austria remained firmly Catholic.

John Calvin

Pope Alexander VI (1492-1503)

The Counter-Reformation

The Catholic Church tried to stop the spread of Protestantism and to put right some of the things that had been wrong with the Church. This movement was called the Counter-Reformation. One of its leaders was Ignatius Loyola who, in 1540, founded the Society of Jesus. The Jesuits, as its members were called, were organized strictly to obey their leader and the Pope without question. In Europe they worked tirelessly to convert Protestants to Catholicism, and their missionaries went to many parts of the world, including China and Japan. Catholicism was also strengthened by the Council of Trent (1545–1563), a Church assembly which made clear what Catholic doctrine was, and reorganized the Church to keep up high standards among the clergy.

As a result of the Counter-Reformation Catholics began to regain lost ground. By 1570, 40 per cent of the people in Europe had become Protestants; by 1650 this was down to 20 per cent. Poland became largely Catholic again, as did France.

Religious Wars

In France, the Netherlands and Germany, Catholic rulers tried to get rid of Protestantism in a series of wars which lasted until 1648. Though the wars were fought in the name of religion, many rulers took part in order to increase their power and territory. In France Queen Catherine de Medici tried to have all the Huguenots (French Calvinists) killed in a great massacre on St Bartholomew's Day in 1572. Many were killed but Protestantism survived. In the Netherlands, Philip II tried to intensify Spanish rule and impose Catholicism, but he was resisted by William of Orange. The Dutch War of Independence against Spain went on for 80 years.

In Central Europe the Habsburg Emperor Ferdinand II began the Thirty Years War (1618–1648), when he brutally crushed Protestants in Bohemia. He seemed likely to defeat all the Protestant princes in Germany, but then King Gustavus Adolphus of Sweden joined in on the side of the Protestants. Gustavus Adolphus saved Protestanism in Germany and won many victories before his death at the battle of Lützen in 1632. Support for German Protestants now came unexpectedly from Catholic France, which wanted to prevent its great rivals, the Habsburgs, from increasing their territories. When the war ended Germany was split into a mainly Protestant north, with Catholic states in the south and west. The divisions in the Christian Church begun by the Reformation remain today.

A scene during the Massacre of St Bartholomew's Day in 1572, when some 29,000 French Protestants were murdered.

CHRONOLOGY
1517 Luther pins his theses to the church door at Wittenberg
1534 The Act of Supremacy makes Henry VIII Head of the Church in England
1540 Loyola founds the Society of Jesus
1541 Geneva becomes a Calvinist city
1545 The Council of Trent first meets
1572 The Massacre of St Bartholomew's Day in France
1598 The Edict of Nantes gives French Protestants freedom of worship
1609 The United Provinces become independent
1632 Death of Gustavus Adolphus at Lützen
1648 Peace of Westphalia ends the Thirty Years War

The Council of Trent met between 1545 and 1563. It consisted of leading members of the Roman Catholic Church. It had two purposes: to get rid of the slack practices of the Church which Luther had criticized, and to set down clearly the teachings of the Church.

THE CHURCH OF ENGLAND
England developed its own kind of Protestantism. Henry VIII wanted a male heir, and his wife had given him only one living child, a daughter. Because the Pope would not give him a divorce, he broke away from the Catholic Church and in 1534 declared himself head of the Church in England. The Anglican Church became established under Queen Elizabeth I and is still the state religion in England.

GERMANY
BOHEMIA
NETHERLANDS
CARPATHIANS
AUSTRIA
HUNGARY
Vienna
Zenta
Mohacs
Danube
Black Sea
Caspian Sea
FRANCE
ALPS
Venice
Milan
Genoa
ITALY
APENNINES
Adriatic Sea
BALKANS
GREECE
Constantinople
ANATOLIA
(TURKEY)
Tigris
Euphrates
Baghdad
SYRIA
PYRENEES
CORSICA
Rome
Naples
Aegean Sea
Gallipoli
Lepanto
Rhodes
CYPRUS
IRAQ
Madrid
SARDINIA
SICILY
CRETE
Jerusalem
SPAIN
Lisbon
Mediterranean Sea
Cairo
EGYPT
Medina
Tunis
TUNISIA
Nile
Red Sea
Mecca
Algiers
Gibraltar
Tripoli
ATLAS MTS
ALGERIA
SAHARA DESERT
Plate from Iznik, Turkey

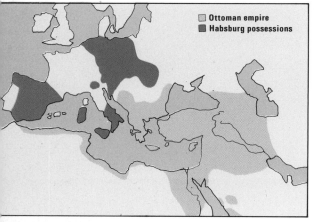

☐ Ottoman empire
■ Habsburg possessions

The Emperor Charles V.

The Mediterranean Area

The Mediterranean was the cradle of European civilization from the time of the Ancient Greeks. The Roman empire was created there and the area kept its importance right up to the Renaissance, when the trade of the Italian city-states such as Venice and Genoa made it the richest area of Europe. In the 16th century Venice and Genoa became less important. Two great powers, the Spanish Habsburgs and the Ottoman Turks, at each end of the Mediterranean, struggled to control it.

The Habsburgs

In 1516 Charles V of the Habsburg family inherited Spain and its Italian lands. Three years later he received the Habsburg lands in Central Europe – Austria and the nearby regions of Germany. In addition his father left him Franche Comté, Luxemburg and the wealthy Netherlands. To crown it all Charles was elected Holy Roman Emperor in 1519. When the new Spanish empire in America was conquered, he ruled a greater empire than anyone since Charlemagne 700 years before. Habsburg power was increased still more when Charles's brother Ferdinand inherited Bohemia and Hungary.

The Valois kings of France were determined to prevent the Habsburgs from dominating Europe. The result was a long series of Valois-Habsburg wars, which began in Italy in 1494. Italy was divided into many states, which made it an easy prey for large, united countries like France and Spain. The wars ended in 1559 with the defeat of France, which left Spain supreme in Italy: it controlled Milan in the north, Naples and Sicily in the south and the island of Sardinia.

Charles gave up his throne in 1556 and divided his territories. The Habsburg lands in Central Europe, together with the title of Holy Roman Emperor, went to his brother Ferdinand, the Spanish lands and the Netherlands to his son Philip II. With its control of southern Italy, Spain was in the front line of defence against the other great Mediterranean power, the Ottoman Turks.

The Ottomans

The Ottomans were originally a band of Turks who moved into Anatolia (Asia Minor) in the 13th century. They took their name from their leader, Osman. They soon ruled over Anatolia, and in the 14th century they gained control of most of the Balkan peninsula. In 1453 Mehmet 'the Conqueror' added to his empire the richest prize of all, the city which had for over a thousand years been the capital of the Byzantine empire – Constantinople.

While Spain gained control of much of Italy on the northern shore of the Mediterranean, the Ottoman Turks were moving along the south. Sultan Selim I (the Grim) defeated the Mamluk rulers of Egypt in 1517. This victory decided the fate of the Near East for the next 400 years, as it gave the Ottomans control not only of Syria, Egypt and Iraq but also of the Muslim holy cities of Mecca and Medina.

SULEYMAN THE MAGNIFICENT

With their Muslim enemies defeated, the Ottoman Turks could now attack Christian Europe again. This was done by Suleyman, who became Sultan in 1520 and ruled till 1566, a long reign which saw the Ottoman empire at the height of its power. In 1522 Suleyman captured the island of Rhodes and then led an expedition across the Danube into Hungary, where he won a great victory at Mohacs in 1526. The fall of Hungary opened the way to the Austrian and German lands, so in 1529 Suleyman advanced towards the imperial capital of Vienna and besieged it. If Vienna had fallen, all Central Europe might have passed under Ottoman control. As it was, the Turks were driven back. This marked the limit of their advance in Europe.

Suleyman besieges Bucharest, in modern Romania.

OTTOMAN DECLINE

In the 17th century the Ottoman threat to Europe grew less. From 1606 to 1639 the Ottomans were fighting the Persians and did not mount a major offensive in Europe, in the grand style, until 1683. Again Vienna was the target and again the Ottomans failed. This failure was final. The Austrians and their allies advanced rapidly into Ottoman territory in Hungary and defeated the Turks at Zenta in 1697. The Turks made peace at Karlowitz and gave up much territory, including most of Hungary, to the Habsburgs. It was the first time the Ottomans had signed a peace as a defeated power and had given up territory. After this the Ottoman empire was all the time on the defensive.

Muslim pirates from North Africa raided shipping in the Mediterranean and the Turks captured southern Greece and Cyprus. In 1571 a Christian fleet defeated a much larger Turkish force at Lepanto (below) but the Turks soon rebuilt their navy.

The World in 1550

Europeans have developed ships, navigational aids and guns which enable them to sail round the world. In doing so they have discovered a new continent, America, where the Spaniards have set up an empire. The Portuguese have sailed to South-East Asia and ended Muslim control of the spice trade. There have been further Muslim setbacks in Russia, where Muscovy has broken away from Mongol control. Elsewhere the Muslims are advancing; the Ottoman threat to Europe is severe, while in India and Persia great Islamic empires are firmly established. In western Europe the Reformation has seen Protestants break away from the Catholic Church. China remains powerful but has little contact with the rest of the world

Western Europe In Germany Luther has begun the Reformation by setting up a 'reformed' Protestant Church. The wars which follow between Catholics and Protestants are still going on but Lutheranism has spread over most of northern Germany and Scandinavia. The ideas of John Calvin, another Protestant reformer, have spread from his native Geneva to Scotland, France and the Netherlands. In Italy the Valois-Habsburg wars (begun in 1494) are still going on, as is the Council of Trent (1545–1563), which strengthens the Catholic Church in its struggle against Protestantism.

At the battle of Panipat in 1526 Babur the Mongol, ruler of Kabul, fought Sultan Ibrahim, the ruler of northern India. Babur was victorious, and Ibrahim and 20,000 of his men were killed. Babur moved on to Delhi where he declared himself emperor. He founded the Mughal empire. Babur himself did not like India much but longed for the hills and streams of Kabul.

The Americas The Aztec civilization has been destroyed by Cortes (1521) and the Inca by Pizarro (1533). Much of North and South America has been explored by Spaniards who by 1550 have followed the Amazon from Peru to its mouth. The French are established in Canada after Jacques Cartier's journey up the St Lawrence river (1535).

Russian dignitary

Tobacco plants

Spanish ivory and gold amulet

Spanish conquistador

Benin plaque of Portuguese trader, West Africa

In 1520 Henry VIII of England met François I of France near Calais at a place known as the Field of Cloth of Gold. Magnificent temporary palaces and pavilions were built for both kings. Henry's alone covered some 10,000 square metres (12,000 square yards) and had a chapel attached. There were several meetings with sumptuous entertainments but no formal alliance was made.

Russia under Ivan IV (the **15** Terrible) is expanding at the expense of the Muslim Khanates on the river Volga.

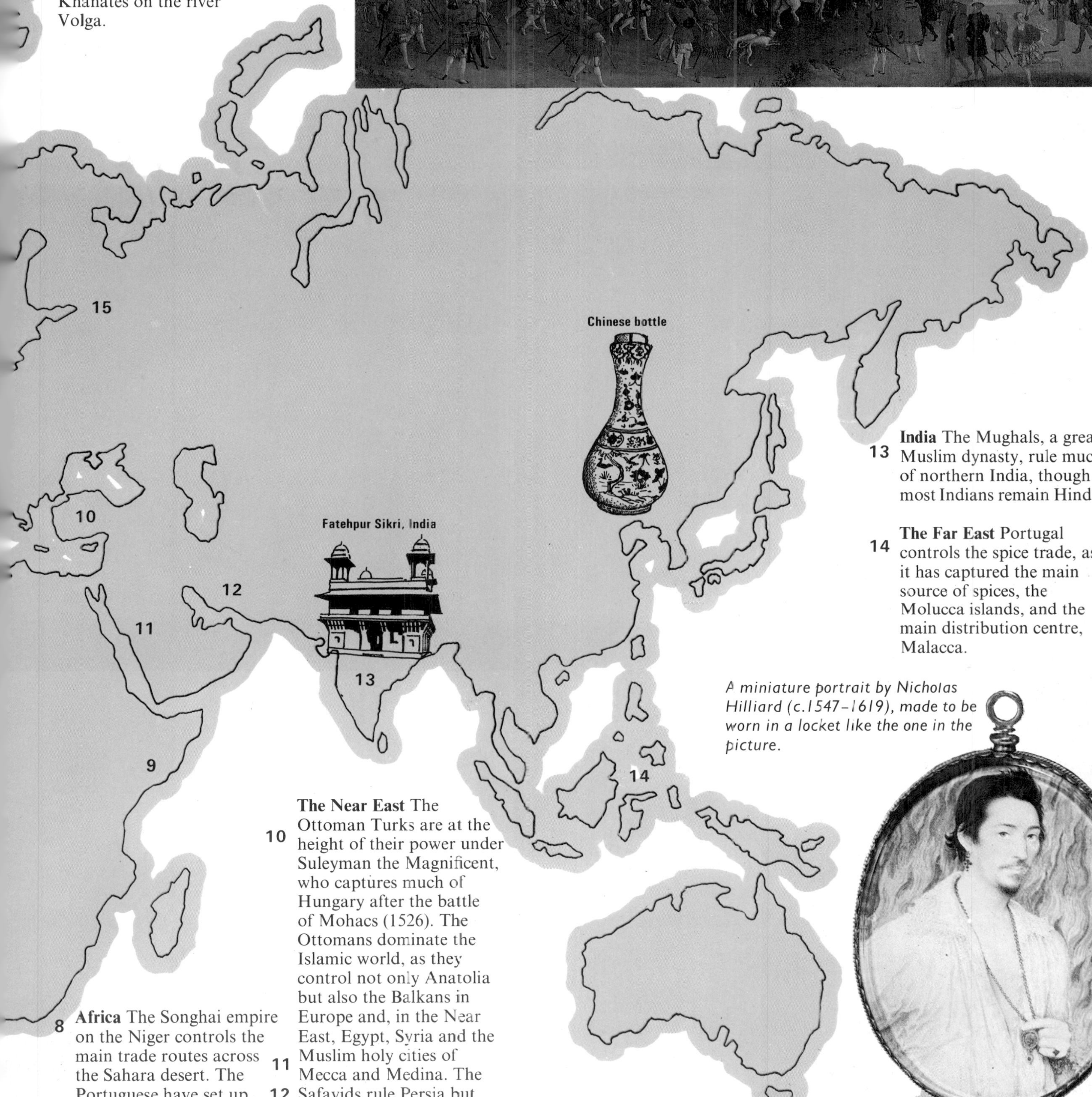

15

Chinese bottle

13 India The Mughals, a great Muslim dynasty, rule much of northern India, though most Indians remain Hindu.

14 The Far East Portugal controls the spice trade, as it has captured the main source of spices, the Molucca islands, and the main distribution centre, Malacca.

Fatehpur Sikri, India

10

12

11

13

9

A miniature portrait by Nicholas Hilliard (c.1547–1619), made to be worn in a locket like the one in the picture.

14

The Near East The **10** Ottoman Turks are at the height of their power under Suleyman the Magnificent, who captures much of Hungary after the battle of Mohacs (1526). The Ottomans dominate the Islamic world, as they control not only Anatolia but also the Balkans in Europe and, in the Near **8 Africa** The Songhai empire East, Egypt, Syria and the on the Niger controls the Muslim holy cities of main trade routes across **11** Mecca and Medina. The the Sahara desert. The Safavids rule Persia but Portuguese have set up **12** spend much time fighting **9** trading posts on the Gold their fellow Muslims, the Coast (Ghana) and in East Ottoman Turks. Africa.

25

The Spread of Islam

Persian rosewater sprinkler
(18th century)

Gold coin of Emperor Jahangir
(17th century)

In 1450 the Muslim world was far larger than the Christian, and Islam went on spreading vigorously after that date. As the Spaniards were conquering an empire in the New World and Portugal was gaining a foothold in India and the East Indies, the Muslim Ottomans were pushing into Central Europe, over-running Hungary. In India the Mughal emperors were steadily moving south until they controlled almost the whole peninsula. In Persia a third great Islamic empire, the Safavid, arose in 1500. Elsewhere the faith of Islam continued to spread in Africa, Central Asia and, with remarkable speed, in Malaya and Indonesia.

The Mughal Empire

In 1504 a group of Turks led by Babur seized Kabul in Afghanistan. Babur claimed descent from Genghis Khan and so was called Mongol, which became Mughal. He invaded the rich plains of India to the south, and at Panipat in 1526 his matchlock muskets and artillery, serviced by Ottoman Turks, enabled his small force of 12,000 men to defeat an Indian army of 100,000. After this victory he occupied Delhi, his new capital, and four years later he died.

Babur's empire survived because of the genius of his grandson, Akbar. A great military leader, he defeated the Hindu Rajputs, conquered the fertile cotton-growing region of Gujarat, and went on to take Bengal. This was the richest province in the north, producing rice and silk, and was Akbar's main source of income. By the time he died his empire stretched from the Bay of Bengal in the east to Afghanistan in the west and included Sind and most of central India. But though the rulers of much of India were now Muslim, less than a fifth of the ordinary people were converted to Islam.

How Islam spread through Asia (left) and Africa.

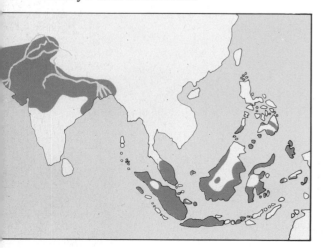

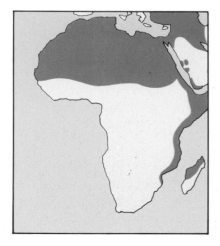

AFRICA AND SOUTH-EAST ASIA

Islam expanded in West Africa and South-East Asia through the missionary work of Muslim traders and holy men. Muslim merchants crossed the Sahara with their camel caravans and converted the people, so that Muslim states grew up in Timbuktu, Kano and Bornu. Muslim Arab traders settled on the east coast. The islands of Indonesia, much of Malaya and parts of Borneo and the Philippines also became Muslim because of the influence of Muslim traders.

26

Safavid Persia

At the same time as Babur was laying the foundations of the Mughal empire, a new dynasty, the Safavid, came to power in Persia (Iran). Its leader was Ismail who captured Tabriz in 1500 and crowned himself Shah. By 1508 all of Persia and most of Iraq were under his control. The Safavid dynasty was to rule Persia for the next 200 years.

The Safavids were Shi'ites, who said that the leaders of Islam should be descended from the family of the Prophet Muhammad. Most Muslims were Sunnis, who believed that the caliph (leader) should be chosen by the Muslim community and need not be descended from Muhammad. This dispute between Sunnis and Shi'ites tore the Muslim world apart, just as the Reformation in Europe led to religious wars between Catholics and Protestants. The Ottomans were Sunnis and fought a long series of wars with the Safavids. These were due both to religious differences and to the desire to possess the same territory.

In 1514 the Ottoman Sultan Selim I (the Grim) advanced into Persia and was victorious, largely because of his use of artillery. He was unable to follow up his victory and conquer the whole of Persia, as he feared attack from Egypt. The division of the Islamic world therefore became permanent. For the rest of the century, except for brief periods, the Ottomans were at war with the Safavids, a war which did not end until 1639.

The Emperor Babur gives instructions to his gardeners. Babur, a fearless warrior, was also a poet and lover of nature. He complained that India had no horses, no grapes or musk melons, no good fruits, no ice or cold water.

DECLINE OF THE MUSLIM EMPIRES

By 1750 Islam was on the defensive. The Ottomans had lost Hungary to the Christian Habsburgs and were no longer powerful enough to threaten Europe. The Safavid dynasty came to an end in Persia in 1736 and the country was ravaged by civil war. In India Aurangzeb (1659–1707) had weakened the Mughal empire by fighting to conquer territory in the south. He left India so low in resources that in the 18th century Muslim fought Hindu, Persians and Afghans invaded from the north-west (the Persians sacked Delhi in 1739) and Europeans seized areas on the coast.

The Safavid dynasty was at its greatest under Shah Abbas the Great (1587–1629) who built a magnificent mosque and palace at Isfahan.

CHRONOLOGY
1500 Ismail captures Tabriz in northern Persia and begins the Safavid dynasty
1504 Babur seizes Kabul in Afghanistan
1514 Ismail is defeated by the Ottoman Turks at Chaldiran
1526 Babur defeats an Indian army at Panipat and conquers northern India
1556 Akbar becomes Mughal Emperor
1574 Akbar captures Bengal (to 1576)
1639 War between Ottomans and Safavids ends
1707 Aurangzeb, last great Mughal Emperor, dies
1736 Safavid dynasty ends

North-West Europe

Dutch man-of-war, 1613

The Armada Medal of Elizabeth I

The remarkable rise to power and prosperity of the Netherlands and England was partly due to their geographical position. England was an island protected by the sea from outside attack: it had never been invaded since 1066. The Netherlands (what are now Belgium and the Kingdom of the Netherlands) stretched across the estuaries of great rivers, the Rhine, Maas and Scheldt. It had excellent harbours and was therefore well placed to be a great trading nation.

Dutch Trade

Dutch prosperity began in the 15th century, when herrings migrated from the Baltic to the North Sea and were caught in great numbers by their fishermen. The Dutch found new methods of preserving and smoking the herrings and exported them to the Baltic, in return for wheat and timber. They also picked up cargoes in Lisbon and Seville from the Spanish and Portuguese empires and took them to Antwerp, where merchants from all over Europe bought them. Antwerp became one of the richest cities and the banking centre of Europe, where kings borrowed money to pay for their wars.

The Dutch invented and built the ideal carrying vessel, the *fluit* or 'flyship'. This was really a sea-going barge, designed to carry bulky goods like grain. It was cheap to build, which was a help in keeping the Dutch freight rates lower than those of other nations.

These merchants' houses in Amsterdam date from the 17th century. It was a time of great prosperity due to the Dutch trading empire.

THE REVOLT OF THE NETHERLANDS

The 17 provinces of the Netherlands were ruled by Spain from 1516. There was no trouble until Philip II became king in 1556 (see page 22). Philip was a devout Catholic and was determined to stamp out Calvinism, which since 1563 had spread to the Netherlands. In 1567 he made the Duke of Alva governor so that he could crush opposition by terror. He began by executing two leaders, Count Egmont and Count Hoorn. A revolt followed which spread more widely as Alva became more ruthless. Public excutions became daily events. Whole towns were pillaged and their populations massacred. In 1576 Antwerp was sacked by Spanish troops and never recovered its former prosperity. This benefitted the north, as many merchants and bankers transferred their business to Amsterdam. After a long struggle, in 1609 Spain had to accept the independence of the seven Protestant northern provinces, known as the United Provinces or Holland. Though war began again, they finally gained their independence in 1648.

By 1680 the Dutch had captured the Portuguese trade to the Spice Islands and built up an empire of their own. Though weakened by a series of naval wars against England (1652–1674) and land wars against France (1672–1713), which a small country with a population of only 2 million could not afford, the United Provinces in 1760 still had a larger share of the carrying trade than any other nation.

England

The English, like the Dutch, became prosperous as a great trading nation. Their sailors gained experience in sailing the oceans by catching cod off Newfoundland, where the seas were teeming with fish. By 1500 sailors from Cornwall and Devon were making regular visits to the fishing grounds there.

The first English to trade with Spanish America took what was most needed there, slaves. In 1562 John Hawkins carried slaves from Sierra Leone to Hispaniola and exchanged them for hides and sugar. These were then sold. The profits were so great that Queen Elizabeth invested in a second voyage. It returned with so much silver that Hawkins became the richest man in England. Hawkins's third expedition in 1567 was attacked by the Spaniards. After that many Englishmen turned from trade to piracy. One of the most successful was Francis Drake.

THE SPANISH ARMADA

England relied on its navy to protect it from foreign attack. The most serious threat came in 1588 when Philip II of Spain prepared to invade England with his Armada. The 130 Spanish ships included many splendid galleons but they were not very manoeuvrable against the wind, as they were tall-sided. The English ships were lower, faster and more manoeuvrable. They fired at short range and avoided the Spanish grappling and boarding tactics. The English broke up the Armada with fire ships at Calais and forced the Spaniards to return home by sailing round Scotland and Ireland, where many were wrecked by storms. After this there was no attempt to invade England until that of Napoleon.

ENGLAND TO BRITAIN

In 1603 Queen Elizabeth I of England died and the throne passed to her cousin, King James VI of Scotland who became James I of England. For over a hundred years the two kingdoms had separate systems of government but in 1707 an Act of Union was passed joining the countries as Great Britain. Scotland was to be represented in the Westminster parliament but was to keep its own legal system and the Scottish Church was to remain independent. From this time on, it is usual to say Britain and the British, rather than England and the English.

The Growth of Industry

In 1500 woollen cloth was England's main export. Nearly all of it went to Europe. Other industries expanded in the next 200 years, including the manufacture of cannon and gunpowder which were in great demand in Europe during the Thirty Years War (1618–1648). The output of coal greatly increased too from 200,000 tonnes in 1550 to 3 million in 1700, as it became more widely used as a fuel. But the increase in trade and industry was mostly due to the English colonies.

From 1651 Navigation Acts made sure that goods carried to or from an English colony must be carried in English ships. As a result England built up a great re-export trade. Goods such as sugar, rum, tobacco and Indian cottons were sent to England and from there were exported to the rest of Europe. The trade increased rapidly. In 1619 Virginia sent only about 9000 kilograms (20,000 pounds) of tobacco to England. By 1700 this had become 10 million kilograms (22 million pounds). The English colonies imported nearly all the manufactures they needed. By 1770 England was exporting more to the colonies than to Europe and the foundations of the Industrial Revolution had been laid.

Francis Drake (1543–1596) is the most famous Elizabethan seaman. He began raiding Spanish colonies in South America in 1572. In 1577 he set off to raid the coast of South America. He captured the treasure ship 'Cacafuego' in the Pacific and made a profit of £1,500,000 on his voyage round the world, the first by an Englishman. On his return Queen Elizabeth knighted him on the deck of his ship 'The Golden Hind'. When the Spaniards prepared to invade England he attacked Cadiz and 'singed the King of Spain's beard' by destroying 33 ships and delaying the Armada for a year. He took part in the battles against the Armada in 1588 and died in 1596 on another search for plunder in the West Indies. He was known to the Spaniards as 'El Draque', the Dragon.

The English fleet chased the Spanish Armada into Calais harbour and anchored to windward of them. Then they sent in fire ships, small craft filled with gunpowder and set alight. The Spaniards cut their anchor cables in panic and drifted hopelessly out of formation. They were defeated by the English at Gravelines.

Colonies in the East

Two countries dominated trade in the Spice Islands of South-East Asia. They were Portugal and the Netherlands. From these islands, known today as Indonesia, they carried astonishingly valuable cargoes back to Europe.

Albuquerque

The Portuguese did not set out to found a great empire. They wanted to control the trade along the spice route, which meant seizing the ports through which the trade passed, as well as the Spice Islands themselves. The man who did this was Afonso de Albuquerque. Although he failed to capture Calicut in India, he took Goa instead in 1510. He made it his main naval base and headquarters. A year later he captured Malacca and in 1515 he took the island of Ormuz at the entrance to the Gulf. Now Portugal controlled the main centres for the collection and distribution of spices. In the Spice Islands the Portuguese captured the Moluccas but never conquered the large islands of Java, Sumatra and

Borneo. Most spices now came to Europe round the Cape of Good Hope but Portugal was not able to close the spice route which went through the Red Sea to the Near East and then to Mediterranean countries. Albuquerque tried to capture Aden, the key to the Red Sea, in 1513 but failed.

Once they were established in South-East Asia, the Portuguese made great profits by trading between Asian ports. With the money from this they were able to buy spices to send to Europe. They acted as carriers for much of the trade between China, Japan and the Philippines. In 1513 they reached Canton, the first Europeans to visit China since Marco Polo. They set up a trading settlement at nearby Macao in 1557. In the 1540s the Portuguese became the first Europeans to land in Japan. Soon they were taking Chinese silk and gold to Japan and bringing back Japanese silver to China. The Portuguese carried on trading with Japan for almost a century, but in the 1630s Japan deliberately cut itself off from contact with other countries. Merchants were forbidden to trade there, except for the Chinese and for one Dutch ship a year.

Albuquerque's ship, 'Frol de la Mar'.

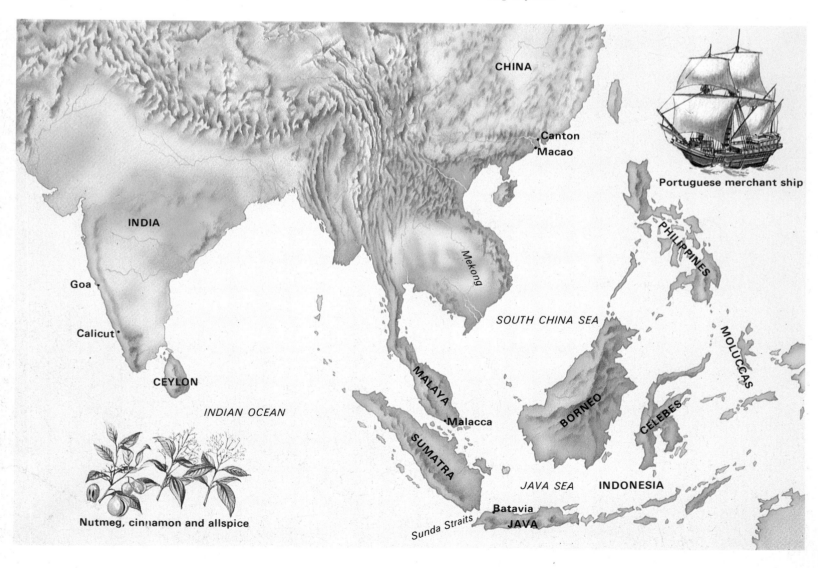

Nutmeg, cinnamon and allspice

Portuguese merchant ship

The Dutch Take Over

During the 16th century the English and Dutch were becoming important naval powers. In the late 1590s both reached the Spice Islands and soon formed East India Companies to start a regular trade. The Dutch wanted to drive the Portuguese from the islands and control the spice trade themselves.

The man who did this was Jan Coen. Between 1618 and 1629 he drove the Portuguese from the Spice Islands and captured Batavia (modern Jakarta, the capital of Indonesia) on the island of Java, which he made his headquarters. Coen also forced the English out of the Spice Islands. His successors captured Malacca (after a six-year blockade, in 1641), Ceylon (1658) and finally the Portuguese forts on the west coast of India but they were not able to capture Goa.

A New Route

The Dutch found a more direct route to the Spice Islands, which meant they did not have to call at Malacca or India. After passing the Cape of Good Hope they sailed due east with the help of westerly winds in the 'roaring forties'. When they reached the area of the south-east trade winds they turned north to the Sunda Straits. After this Malacca became less important and fewer spices went to the Red Sea and the Gulf.

The kind of goods carried by the Dutch also changed. At first spices were the most valuable cargoes brought to Holland, but by 1700 Indian cotton goods were more important. After 1700 tea and coffee were most valuable. The Dutch introduced coffee bushes into Java and forced the farmers there to grow coffee, tea, sugar and tobacco. In 1711 they produced 45 kilograms (100 pounds) of coffee; by 1723 this had risen to over 5 million kilograms (12 million pounds). Coffee became a popular drink in Europe and the Dutch were the main suppliers.

Like the Portuguese before them, the Dutch carried goods between different parts of Asia, a trade which was much larger and more valuable than the trade with Europe. After the Japanese expelled the Portuguese from Japan in 1639, the Dutch were the only Europeans allowed to trade there, a position they held for over 200 years.

The Dutch were never able to control all the trade in the Indian Ocean, as they had no strong base on the coast of India. In the wars against Louis XIV of France, which did not end until 1713, they had to spend most of their wealth on their army. The navy was neglected. As a result England, Holland's great rival at sea, was able to take control of India.

This ivory cabinet, mounted with silver, was made in Ceylon in about 1700. The scenes, showing Adam and Eve, were copied from a Dutch engraving.

This drawing of Batavia (modern Jakarta) in Java was made in Amsterdam in 1682. It was an important port of call for European traders.

CHRONOLOGY

1510 Albuquerque captures Goa and Malacca (1511)
1513 Portuguese reach Canton
1515 The Portuguese capture Ormuz at the entrance to the Gulf
1557 Portuguese set up trading settlement at Macao
1564 Spain establishes a colony in the Philippines
1602 Dutch East India Company formed
1605 Dutch drive Portuguese from the Molucca Islands
1619 Coen captures Batavia
1629 Dutch drive the Portuguese from the Spice Islands (Indonesia)
1638 Dutch begin conquest of Ceylon
1639 Portuguese expelled from Japan
1641 Dutch seize Malacca
1713 End of Dutch wars against Louis XIV of France

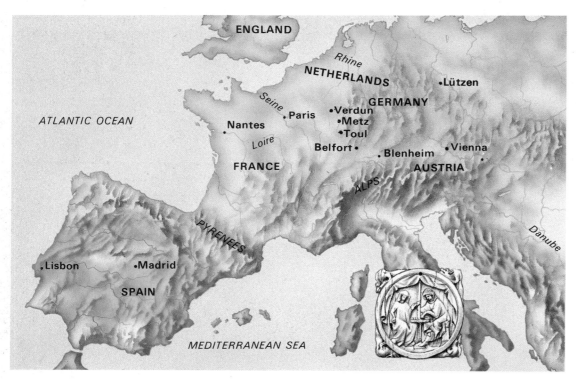

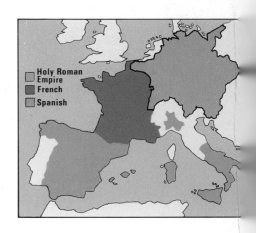

A Struggle for Power

In the early 17th century Europe was torn by religious conflicts. After these came to an end a new issue arose: the struggle for dominance between France and the Holy Roman Empire, the two most powerful states. When the king of Spain died without children, the ruling families of both states had a claim to the vacant throne, and in the resulting war many lesser states were involved.

Louis XIV's magnificent palace at Versailles.

'Le Roi Soleil'

Louis XIV became king of France in 1643 at the age of five. For many years the real ruler of France was Cardinal Mazarin. On the day after Mazarin's death in 1661 the 22-year-old King called his ministers together and told them that he intended to rule personally. 'From now on you will not make any decisions, or sign any papers, except on my orders.' In his *Mémoires* he later wrote: 'The one emotion which overpowers all others in the minds of kings is the sense of their own greatness and glory.'

Louis XIV is known in France as *le grand monarque* (the great king) and the time in which he lived as *le grand siècle* (the great century). He would not have disagreed, as he took for his symbol the Sun, *le soleil*, which casts its light on all the world. He was also known as *le roi soleil*, the Sun King.

In 1661 France needed strong leadership, as the country was exhausted by the recent rebellion of the nobility, known as the Fronde. Louis worked hard at governing France but for this he needed large sums of money. Fortunately, France was a large and fertile kingdom with a population of 20 million. His minister of finance, Colbert, did much to build up France's strength. He created new industries, promoted commerce, increased the navy and improved roads and canals. The Languedoc Canal, completed in 1681, was the first great canal in Europe since Roman times and carried goods from the Atlantic to the Mediterranean. France also had its trading companies and colonies in the West Indies and Canada.

Some of Colbert's work was undone in 1685, when Louis ended the freedom of worship which Protestants (called Huguenots) had enjoyed since the Edict of Nantes in 1598. Many including skilled craftsmen and merchants fled abroad.

DEFENDING THE FRONTIERS

Under Louis XIV France became so powerful that other countries feared it would dominate Europe. Louis's aims were more limited and were concerned with the security of France's northern and eastern frontiers. He felt that the Habsburgs pressed like a ring round France which could be invaded from the Spanish Netherlands (modern Belgium) in the north, Lorraine and the Belfort gap in the east, and the Barcelonette valley from Italy. Spain still held Franche Comté on France's east. To protect his frontiers, Louis waged a series of wars from 1667 to 1697.

The battle of Blenheim, in which the Duke of Marlborough and Prince Eugene of Savoy led the English and Austrian forces to victory over the French. Above: The English attack the village of Blenheim; below: Prince Eugene's troops attack the French. This battle was a terrible blow to French pride. It saved Vienna and ended Louis's hopes of defeating Austria.

THE PALACE OF VERSAILLES

Versailles was designed to provide a suitable setting for *le roi soleil*, the Sun King. An enormous amount of money was spent on the finest materials, architects, craftsmen, painters and sculptors. It was vast in size – the front was 415 metres (1361 feet) and the Hall of Mirrors 73 metres (240 feet) long. Behind the palace were extensive gardens and a park.

Louis made Versailles the centre of European culture; there the comedies of Molière could be seen or the operas of Lully heard. The main attraction was Louis himself and the elaborate ceremonial of the court.

There was little comfort in the palace. Both courtiers and servants were crowded into tiny, dark, airless rooms. The plumbing was poor and baths almost unheard of. Instead, men and women splashed themselves freely with perfume.

Louis XIV, who ruled France for over 70 years.

The Spanish Succession

France's main enemy was the Habsburg rulers of the Holy Roman Empire. The Empire itself had been threatened from the east by the Ottoman Turks. In 1683 Vienna was besieged by the Turks and was saved only by the timely appearance of John Sobieski, King of Poland. From then on the Habsburgs took the offensive and won a crushing victory over the Turks at Zenta in Serbia in 1697. When peace was made two years later the Emperor was free to turn his attention to the west – to France.

It was certain that Charles II of Spain would die without children. This meant that the Spanish and Austrian Habsburg lands might be united again, as they had been under the Emperor Charles V (see page 22). As the Spanish lands included Spanish America, the Netherlands and parts of Italy, this would have made the Habsburgs the dominant power in Europe. Louis XIV could not accept this. He had a claim to the Spanish throne himself, through his wife and mother. The War of the Spanish Succession was a struggle between France and Austria over who was to rule Spain.

England, as usual, fought against its old enemy France, as one of Austria's allies. When the French boldly tried to march on Vienna they were thwarted by the Duke of Marlborough, who joined up with the army of Prince Eugene of Savoy at Blenheim in Bavaria. Here the French suffered their first great military defeat, in 1704. The war dragged on until 1711, when the Austrian Emperor died. The Archduke Charles, the Habsburg candidate for the Spanish throne, now became Emperor. If he became King of Spain too there would be the same situation the Allies had tried to avoid – the union of Spain with one of the great powers of Europe. It was agreed, therefore, at the Peace of Utrecht in 1713 that the Spanish empire should be divided up. Philip of Anjou, a Bourbon prince, would become Philip V of Spain but the thrones of France and Spain would never be united. Austria received the Spanish lands in Italy and the Netherlands.

The result of all these wars was that the balance of power was preserved – no one state dominated Europe.

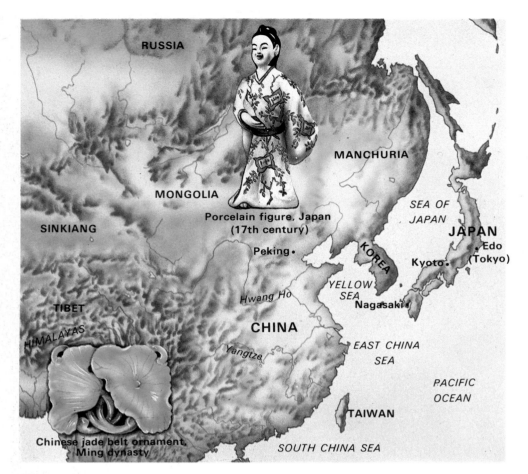

Porcelain figure, Japan
(17th century)

Chinese jade belt ornament,
Ming dynasty

China and Japan

In much of Asia Europeans easily defeated local rulers, but in the Far East they faced two powerful empires, China and Japan. In 1450 China was a greater military force than the whole of Europe. Until new weapons and the Industrial Revolution brought greater strength to the Europeans, they could not hope to conquer either empire.

In the 12th century Mongols invaded China from the north and took control of the whole country. In 1368 they were overthrown by the native Chinese Ming dynasty (ruling family), whose name means 'clear' or 'brilliant'. Under the Ming, China became powerful. The population grew rapidly from 100 to 150 million, as new crops including maize, peanuts and the sweet potato were brought in from America. The sweet potato could be grown in poor soils and on hillsides where rice would not grow. Cotton spinning and weaving brought fresh wealth to the rich cities of the Yangtze valley. A splendid new capital, Peking, grew up, and a canal was cut to link it with the Yangtze.

A 17th-century drawing of ambassadors at the Meridian Gate, Peking. There were four walled cities at Peking, each surrounded by great walls. Most people lived in the Outer City. To its north was the Inner City, within which was the Imperial City where the most important members of the government lived. Within the Imperial City was the Forbidden City, which few people could enter. Here lived the imperial family.

The Manchus

The Ming emperors became unpopular because of heavy and unjust taxation. Rebellions all over China allowed a nomadic tribe from the north, the Manchus, to seize Peking in 1644. They set up a new dynasty, the Ch'ing (meaning 'pure'). The Manchus were to rule until the empire collapsed in 1911. They soon restored peace and order and accepted Chinese ways. They relied on Chinese civil servants to run the empire but kept the leadership of the army in their own hands.

Trade boomed, and Chinese silk, tea, cotton goods and porcelain (known as 'china' in Europe) went overland to Russia and by sea to other parts of the world. Chinese styles and designs were very popular in Europe in the 17th and 18th centuries. The growing taste for tea-drinking in Europe in the 18th century led to a big new export trade.

A great task facing all Chinese dynasties was to control the barbarian tribes on the northern frontier. Here the mounted archers of the steppe were difficult to defeat until firearms were introduced. The Manchus began a long series of campaigns which, between 1688 and 1757, added Mongolia and the vast region of Sinkiang to the empire. Tibet was made a protectorate, and remained so until it became independent, briefly, in 1912. The Chinese also drove the Russians out of the Amur valley. On its other borders most states, including Korea, Annam, Burma, and Siam (Thailand) paid a yearly tribute to China, but were left to govern themselves. The Chinese empire had never been as extensive and apparently secure as it was in 1757.

Tokugawa Japan

For over a century from 1467 there was confusion in Japan. There was no effective government and the great lords fought among themselves. The fighting ended in 1603 when Ieyasu, a member of the Tokugawa family, was made *shogun* (military leader) by the emperor.

As the emperor was supposed to be descended from the Sun goddess (the Sun is still Japan's national symbol) he was sacred. As a result there has been only one ruling family in Japan: the present emperor is descended from the earliest emperors. In theory he was all-powerful but real control belonged to the shogun.

The Tokugawas set up their capital at Edo, later called Tokyo. This was a small fishing village, which they made into an enormous fortress-city. By 1721 Tokyo had a population of 800,000, the largest of any city in the world. There the Tokugawas established a strong, efficient dictatorship. The shogun compelled the great lords to spend a lot of time at his court, where he could keep an eye on them. When they returned to their own estates, they had to leave their wives and children at court as hostages. No revolution threatened the peace and order of Tokugawa rule for 250 years.

A well-known figure in 16th-century Japan was the 'samurai' or mounted warrior. Samurai prided themselves on their toughness and self-discipline and preferred death to dishonour or capture. But in 1542 muzzle-loading muskets were introduced into Japan and in battles such as this infantry with firearms were able to defeat the samurai, still armed with their traditional weapons.

This flask of cloisonné enamel was made in China in the early 17th century.

THE 'CHRISTIAN CENTURY'

For a time Japan's contact with Europe was much greater than that of China, and the period from the 1540s to the 1630s has been called the 'Christian Century'.

The first Portuguese ship reached Japan in 1542. Merchants were followed by missionaries, who were able to make many converts to Christianity (150,000 by 1580). The shogun regarded this as a dangerous threat to Japanese beliefs, so there was a brief, violent and successful persecution of Christians, all of whom were put to death. By 1650 Christianity was almost completely wiped out in Japan.

Not only missionaries were kept out of Japan. In the 1630s foreign merchants were forbidden to trade there, except for the Dutch, who were allowed to send one ship a year to Nagasaki, and the Chinese. The Japanese were forbidden to trade abroad or to build large, ocean-going ships. This cut off Japan from contact with other countries until 1854.

Christian missionaries are tortured by the Japanese; they were looked on as a serious threat to Japanese religious beliefs.

Gustavus Adolphus of Sweden was known as the Lion of the North. An inspiring leader and a splendid horseman, he loved danger and was always first in the attack. He modernized the Swedish army and made Sweden the greatest military power in the north.

The Baltic Region

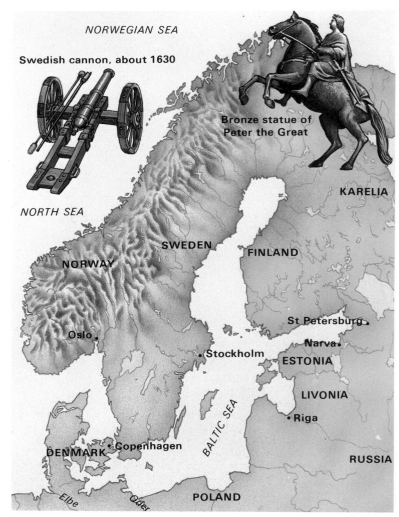

The Baltic is a large, almost land-locked sea, parts of which are covered with ice in the winter. In the 15th and 16th centuries the area around it provided most of the timber, tar and hemp which sea-going nations like Spain, Portugal, the Netherlands, England and France needed to build their ships. From the Baltic also came most of the grain which was eaten in western Europe, and the copper which was used for its money. Ships carrying these goods had to pass through the narrow Sound between Denmark and Sweden to reach the North Sea, and paid tolls there. This made Denmark, which usually controlled the Sound, very wealthy but it made its neighbours jealous and led to a series of wars.

The Rise of Sweden

From 1397 until 1523 Denmark, Norway and Sweden were united. Then Sweden became independent. The Swedes wanted to be a strong naval and military power but they had enemies on all sides: Denmark, Poland and Russia (who wanted Finland, under Swedish control).

In 1611 the 17-year-old Gustavus Adolphus became king of Sweden and during his reign he was to do a great deal to control the Baltic like a Swedish lake. His army was the best equipped, trained and disciplined since the Romans. In 1617 he took Ingermanland and Karelia and so cut off Russia from the Baltic. Next he extended Sweden's territories on the southern shore of the Baltic to include Livonia. He was killed at Lützen in 1632, but this Swedish victory confirmed that Sweden was the greatest military power in the north. It gained even more territory in north Germany at the Peace of Westphalia, which ended the Thirty Years War in 1648. Ten years later Sweden had pushed its territory to the northern shore of the Sound, so that Denmark no longer controlled both sides of the seaway. Fear of Sweden led its enemies to join together against it. Foremost among these was Russia, under Peter the Great.

Peter the Great

For over 200 years following the Mongol conquest of 1237, Russia had been cut off from all contact with the rest of Europe. Its rulers realized how much it lagged behind other countries in technical skills. Tsars like Ivan III and Ivan the Terrible wanted firearms and artillery from the West, and foreign officers to train their army. Peter the Great speeded up this process by forcing his people to copy western customs. He ordered Russians to shave off their beards and forbade them to wear the big Russian cloak. He himself travelled in disguise to England and Holland, where he worked as a labourer in the shipyards to learn about shipbuilding. He wanted to make Russia strong and above all, he wanted a 'window on the West'.

The Great Northern War

Russia's coastline in the Arctic made trade with Europe difficult, as the White Sea was frozen for a large part of the year. In the south the Ottomans and Crimean Tartars kept Russians from the Black Sea. Peter was determined to gain a foothold on the Baltic and recklessly attacked Sweden, with Denmark and Poland, before he had time to build a western-style army. In 1700 a large Russian army was defeated at Narva by a much smaller Swedish force. Fortunately for Peter, Charles XII of Sweden turned aside from Russia and spent the next six years fighting in Poland and Saxony. While Charles was occupied there Peter reorganized his army. He introduced conscription (one person in every 20 households had to serve for 25 years, a system that lasted until 1874) and based his training and tactics on German, French and Swedish models.

When Charles XII had completed his conquest of Poland and Saxony he turned to Russia. His aim was to strike at Moscow. The Russians avoided a pitched battle and used a 'scorched-earth' policy, retreating before the invaders and destroying everything they could not take with them, so that the Swedish army could not live off the land. Charles, therefore, turned to the rich country of the Ukraine, but there many of his men died in the bitter winter of 1708–1709. Finally, in 1709, Peter totally defeated Charles' diminished army at Poltava. The whole position in northern Europe was changed. Peter went on to capture the Swedish provinces, including south-east Finland, Estonia and Livonia, on the Baltic coast and his influence replaced that of Sweden in Poland. Sweden also lost most of its territories in north Germany.

This marked the end of one major power in the north, Sweden, and the rise of another, Russia. For the first time Russia was feared by her neighbours. 'It is commonly said,' wrote the contemporary German philosopher Leibniz, 'that the Tsar will be formidable to all Europe, that he will be a kind of Northern Turk.'

The port of Archangel on the White Sea, north-east of Karelia, was the only Russian seaport before the building of St Petersburg. The town began when the English Muscovy Company built a trading station there in the late 16th century. In the winter the harbour froze over.

ST PETERSBURG

In 1703 Peter began to build a new city on land taken from Sweden at the mouth of the river Neva (a Finnish word for 'swamp'). It was a damp, unhealthy site, with dark, long and very cold winters. While building St Petersburg, as it was called after him, 200,000 labourers died from cold and fever. It was to be Peter's 'window on the west', a city built by French, Dutch, German and Italian architects. It was a great symbol of the new Russia, just as Moscow, with its onion domes, was of the old. 'We have lifted the curtain of our country's curiosity', he said, 'which deprived it of communication with the whole world.' He made it his new capital in 1712, and it remained the capital of the Russian empire for over 200 years. It is now renamed Leningrad.

The World in 1650

The century-long religious wars between Catholics and Protestants end with the Thirty Years War (1618–1648), which has brought ruin and famine to Germany. The 1640s have been a period of turmoil in Europe, with civil war in England and France; the Dutch and Portuguese have gained independence from Spain. In the north, Sweden controls the Baltic; unnoticed in the west, Russia is expanding across Siberia and has already reached the Pacific. In the East, too, there have been upheavals. In China a new dynasty, the Ch'ing, has replaced the Ming; Japan has been united, after a century of civil war, by the Tokugawa family. The Portuguese have lost most of their eastern empire to the Dutch.

The Americas In the north, the English, French, and
1 Dutch have begun to colonize the Atlantic coast of North America. Spanish colonies in Central and
2 South America send vast quantities of silver and gold to Europe; Brazil, under the Portuguese, is
3 important as a sugar producer.

Northern Europe Civil war in England has ended in the execution of Charles I (1649) and the setting up of a Commonwealth (Republic). The seven
5 northern provinces of the Netherlands are finally independent of Spain.
6 Germany is divided into a mainly Protestant north and a Catholic south and west. In the Baltic region
7 Sweden is the leading power.

Western Europe France is
4 suffering from civil war (the *Fronde*) in which nobles try to prevent an increase in the power of the king. Spain has declined, following years of war with France, and Portugal has regained independence in 1640 after 60 years of Spanish rule.

Louis XIV of France looks at plans for his palace at Versailles.

Puritan settlers, Massachusetts

Isaac Newton's telescope of 1672

Benin head, West Africa

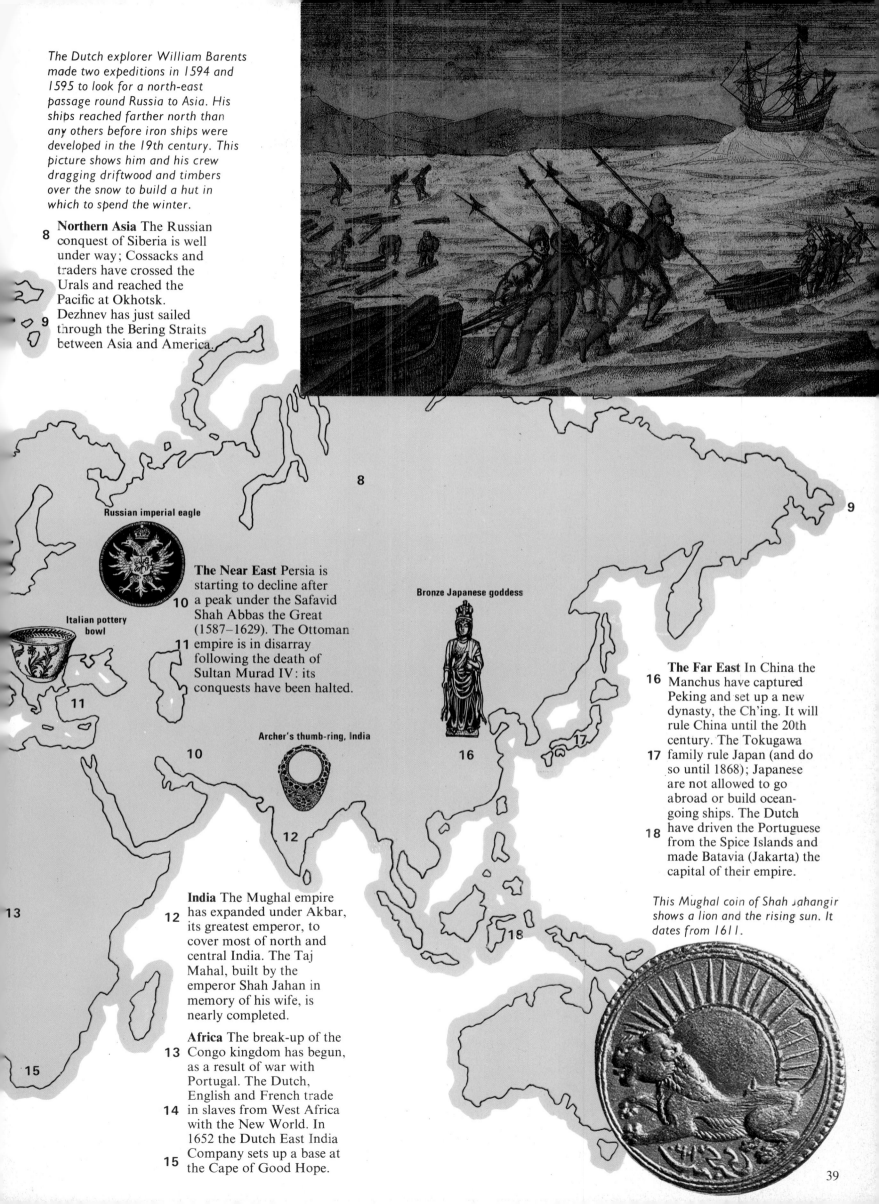

The Dutch explorer William Barents made two expeditions in 1594 and 1595 to look for a north-east passage round Russia to Asia. His ships reached farther north than any others before iron ships were developed in the 19th century. This picture shows him and his crew dragging driftwood and timbers over the snow to build a hut in which to spend the winter.

8 Northern Asia The Russian conquest of Siberia is well under way; Cossacks and traders have crossed the Urals and reached the Pacific at Okhotsk. **9** Dezhnev has just sailed through the Bering Straits between Asia and America.

Russian imperial eagle

Italian pottery bowl

The Near East Persia is starting to decline after **10** a peak under the Safavid Shah Abbas the Great (1587–1629). The Ottoman **11** empire is in disarray following the death of Sultan Murad IV: its conquests have been halted.

Bronze Japanese goddess

Archer's thumb-ring, India

The Far East In China the **16** Manchus have captured Peking and set up a new dynasty, the Ch'ing. It will rule China until the 20th century. The Tokugawa **17** family rule Japan (and do so until 1868); Japanese are not allowed to go abroad or build ocean-going ships. The Dutch **18** have driven the Portuguese from the Spice Islands and made Batavia (Jakarta) the capital of their empire.

This Mughal coin of Shah Jahangir shows a lion and the rising sun. It dates from 1611.

India The Mughal empire **12** has expanded under Akbar, its greatest emperor, to cover most of north and central India. The Taj Mahal, built by the emperor Shah Jahan in memory of his wife, is nearly completed.

Africa The break-up of the **13** Congo kingdom has begun, as a result of war with Portugal. The Dutch, English and French trade **14** in slaves from West Africa with the New World. In 1652 the Dutch East India Company sets up a base at **15** the Cape of Good Hope.

North America

At one time there were four colonial powers in North America. The Spaniards gradually moved from Mexico into Texas and up the west coast to California. By 1767 Spain claimed territory as far east as the river Mississippi and as far north as San Francisco. They stopped only when they met the Russians, moving down the Pacific coast from Alaska. The Dutch founded New Amsterdam (later New York) in 1612. It was a thriving base for exporting furs which came down the Hudson river. It was also a centre for Dutch trade with the Spanish, English and French colonies in America. Because of this the English captured it in 1664. The main struggle for control of North America was between England and France.

Carved wooden thunderbird, Canada

Hudson's ship 'Half Moon'

Anglo-French Rivalry

French explorers like Jacques Cartier had sailed up the St Lawrence river by 1535. They built ports in Nova Scotia, Quebec and Montreal. From the St Lawrence they pushed west by water to Lake Superior and south to the river Ohio. In 1682 La Salle paddled down the Mississippi to the Gulf of Mexico and claimed the whole river basin for France. He called it Louisiana, after King Louis XIV. The French had reached the heart of North America and circled the English colonies on the seaboard by building forts from the St Lawrence to Louisiana.

English colonization first began successfully with the founding of Jamestown, Virginia in 1607, and with the Pilgrim fathers in the *Mayflower* who landed in Massachusetts Bay in 1620. By 1700 there were 12 English colonies on or near the Atlantic coast of America (Georgia was added in 1733). It was clear that when the English crossed the Appalachian mountains they would clash with the French.

In both the French and English colonies there were few Indians, so the colonists could not use Indian labour, as the Spaniards had done in South America. Unlike the Spaniards, the English and French found no gold or silver, so they had to make a living by agriculture, fishing and the fur trade. Virginia was an exception; here the colonists grew tobacco and exported it in large quantities to Europe.

More Englishmen than Frenchman emigrated to America. By 1688 there were 250,000 Englishmen on the Atlantic coast, compared with only 20,000 Frenchmen in the vast area of Canada and the Mississippi valley. By 1760 there were over 2 million Englishmen; Massachusetts alone had as many settlers as New France. This largely explains the victory of the English over the French in their American wars.

The city of Quebec in 1754, seen from a ferry house across the St Lawrence river. At this time the city was French, but five years later it was captured by the British, during the Seven Years War. Under General Wolfe a British force scaled the cliffs to the Plains of Abraham (on the left) and took the French by surprise. Both Wolfe and the French commander Montcalm were killed.

An Indian chief, probably in ceremonial attire, drawn in about 1585. As French and English settlers moved westwards into the interior of North America and took over the most fertile lands they came increasingly into conflict with the Indian tribes.

Below: Bacons Castle, Virginia, was built in 1655. The Virginia Company was given a charter by King James I in 1606 and sent colonists to establish the first permanent English settlement there in 1607. Soon the colonists were growing and exporting tobacco and in 1624 Virginia was made a royal colony.

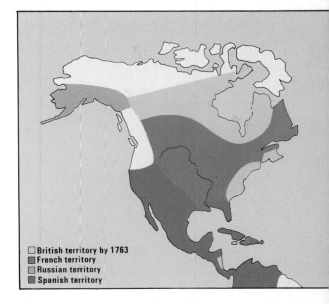

☐ British territory by 1763
☐ French territory
☐ Russian territory
☐ Spanish territory

Anglo-French Wars

The struggle between England and France in America began early. Quebec was first attacked by the English in 1629 and Nova Scotia changed hands many times. Each war between England and France in Europe was fought in America too. The Peace of Utrecht in 1713 gave Britain Nova Scotia, Newfoundland and a large area round Hudson Bay. The main war which decided the fate of North America was the French and Indian War of 1754 to 1760, which became part of the Seven Years' War in Europe.

The war began as a struggle for control of the Ohio valley. British settlers were moving across the mountains into the valley and built a fort in 1754 where the Monongahela and Allegheny rivers meet. The French immediately captured it and named it Fort Duquesne. A young Virginian, George Washington, hurried to reinforce the English garrison but arrived too late. In 1755 General Braddock with a British army tried to recapture Fort Duquesne but was defeated and killed. The French continued to do well through the brilliant leadership of the Marquis de Montcalm, probably the finest general on either side, until William Pitt (later Earl of Chatham) became the English Prime Minister. He left his ally, Frederick the Great of Prussia, to fight the French in Europe and concentrated on the navy and the war in the colonies. His policy succeeded. The British navy controlled the seas, while a large force of 50,000 British soldiers and American colonists was formed. They captured one French fort after another, including Fort Duquesne, which they renamed Fort Pitt (now Pittsburgh). The climax came with the capture of Quebec in 1759 and of Montreal in 1760. This was the end of the French empire in America.

In the Peace of Paris, which ended the war, France lost Canada and most of its American possessions. It kept only French Guiana in South America, the islands of St Pierre and Miquelon off the Newfoundland coast and the West Indian sugar islands of Guadeloupe and Martinique. Britain gained the St Lawrence valley and all territory east of the Mississippi. Spain had entered the war late on the side of France and gave up Florida to Britain. As compensation, France gave Spain western Louisiana, territory west of the Mississippi. North America was now to develop as part of the English-, rather than the French-speaking, world.

THE FALL OF QUEBEC

Quebec was a great natural stronghold defended by Montcalm. It seemed impossible to capture, as cliffs rose straight up from the banks of the St Lawrence. The British commander, 33-year-old General Wolfe, tried a daring plan. At night on September 13 1759, he silently ferried his troops upstream, where they climbed the steep paths up the cliffs and reached the Plains of Abraham above the town. At dawn Montcalm was surprised to see a red-coated British army on the Plains. He attacked immediately. In less than an hour the French were defeated; both Wolfe and Montcalm were killed. Quebec fell five days later.

Map labels: BERING STRAITS, Ivan the Terrible, ARCTIC TUNDRA, Lena, Tungus tribesmen, Yenisei, WHITE SEA, Archangel, Okhotsk, Neva, MUSCOVY, Ob, Yakutsk, St Petersburg (Leningrad), STANOVOI MTS, Moscow, URAL MTS, Sibir, SIBERIA, Amur, PACIFIC OCEAN, RUSSIA, Kazan, Volga, Irtysh, Astrakhan, CASPIAN SEA, MONGOLIA, CHINA, TIBET

Russia in Asia

At the same time as western Europeans were moving overseas to all corners of the world, the Russians were advancing overland across the whole length of Asia. Russia today is a vast country, which covers one sixth of the Earth's land surface. When night falls in Leningrad (St Petersburg) on the Baltic, day is breaking in Vladivostok on the Pacific 8000 kilometres (5000 miles) away. Most of Russia is a flat plain. The Ural Mountains run across it from north to south and are usually taken as the dividing line between European and Asiatic Russia, but they are a narrow, worn-down chain of mountains with an average height of only 600 metres (2000 feet). This explains why the Russians were able to move eastwards so easily into the area called Siberia.

The Land of Russia

The main divisions of Russia do not stretch from north to south but from east to west. In the north along the Arctic is the barren tundra, frozen for most of the year. Below this is the forest belt. Farther south is the fertile soil of the open steppe or grasslands. The southern boundary is a chain of mountains, deserts and inland seas. These mountains keep out the moisture-laden winds from the Pacific and the Indian Ocean and are the cause of the deserts of Central Asia and the cold, dry climate of

Siberia. The whole of Siberia has the same climate; short, hot summers and long, cold winters. Russian settlers therefore felt equally at home anywhere in the plains.

Because the land is flat, Russian rivers are generally long, wide and have few rapids. East of the Urals, there are four great rivers: the Ob, Yenisei, Lena and Amur. As Siberia slopes down from the huge mountains of Tibet, all these rivers flow north except for the Amur, which flows into the Pacific. Using these rivers and their tributaries, Russian explorers and settlers could move almost all the way across Siberia by water. This made trade and conquest easier.

A view of Moscow in the time of Ivan the Terrible.

The Defeat of The Mongols

When the Mongols conquered Russia the Russians retreated from the steppe deep into the forest belt, where the state of Muscovy, based on the city of Moscow, grew up. Ivan III declared his independence of the Mongols in 1480, overcame rival Russian princes and took the title of *tsar*, (the Russian form of 'caesar'). There was still much fighting to do before Ivan IV 'the Terrible' defeated the Mongols. Ivan was able to capture Kazan in 1552, because he had better artillery and the help of a Dane who mined and blew up the walls of the fortress. When the Russians captured Astrakhan at the mouth of the Volga, they controlled the whole Volga basin to the Caspian Sea. The way was now open for expansion across the Urals.

The conquest of Siberia was largely the work of rough frontiersmen, called Cossacks. Siberia was thinly populated, so there was little effective resistance to the Russians with their firearms. They were lured on by the search for furs – sable, squirrel and ermine. As they advanced the Cossacks built fortified posts or *ostrogs*. They built one at Yakutsk on the river Lena in 1632 and moved out from there in all directions. Some Russians reached the Arctic in 1645 and the Pacific two years later, at Okhotsk. In 1648 Semion Dezhnev set out from Yakutsk down the Lena, which was so broad in places that he could not see either bank. He reached the Arctic and sailed east to the tip of Asia. Then he sailed through the Bering Straits, which separate America from Asia, 77 years before Vitus Bering after whom the straits are named.

China and The Amur

The Russians met their first serious opposition when they moved south into the Amur valley. This territory was claimed by China. When the Cossacks pillaged the area the Chinese sent an expedition which forced the Russians to withdraw. The Chinese and the Russians settled their frontier problems by the Treaty of Nerchinsk in 1689. This was the first treaty signed by China with a European country. The frontier was fixed along the Stanovoi mountains north of the Amur, so the Russians had to pull out of the whole valley. In return the Russians were given permission to trade with China. Caravans took gold and furs to China and brought back tea, which soon became the national drink in Russia.

With the Treaty of Nerchinsk the first stage of Russian expansion in Asia ended. Russia did not continue its advance south until the middle of the 19th century.

Top: The valley of the river In'a in Siberia. Above: These Tungus tribespeople, from central Siberia, were drawn on a map of 1729 showing the explorations of Vitas Bering.

YERMAK

Yermak was the red-bearded son of a Don Cossack and a Danish slave woman. Condemned to death at the age of 21 for stealing horses, he fled to the Volga and became a river pirate. He was then hired by a wealthy merchant to stop raids by Siberian Tartars (Mongols) from across the Urals, led by the blind Khan Kuchum. In 1581 Yermak set off with 840 men to attack the Khan. He had firearms and cannon, which terrified the natives. Kuchum had far more men and fought desperately but in vain to save his capital, Sibir. When Yermak occupied Sibir the Russians gave its name to the entire area across the Urals – Siberia. Ivan the Terrible was so pleased with Yermak that he pardoned him for his earlier crimes. In 1584 one of Kuchum's raiding parties surprised Yermak who tried to escape by swimming across a river. He drowned, according to legend, under the weight of armour given to him by the Tsar.

CHRONOLOGY

1237 The Mongols begin the conquest of Russia
1480 Ivan III declares his independence of the Mongols
1552 Ivan the Terrible captures Kazan
1556 Astrakhan seized; Ivan now controls the whole of the Volga, Russia's longest river
1581 Yermak crosses the Urals; captures Sibir
1584 Port of Archangel founded on the White Sea
1632 Ostrog (fort) built at Yakutsk
1645 Russians sail down the Lena to reach the Arctic
1647 The Pacific reached at Okhotsk
1648 Dezhnev begins journey which leads to discovery of the Bering Straits
1689 Treaty of Nerchinsk; Russians withdraw from the Amur valley

Africa

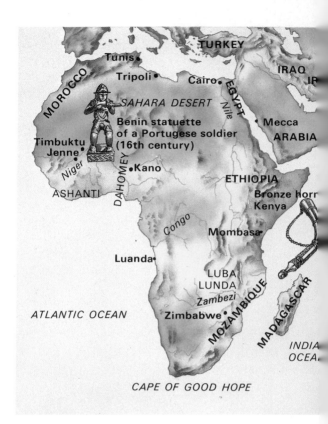

The Mediterranean connects the peoples of North Africa with others round its shores. But the Sahara Desert with its trackless, burning dunes cuts off people to the south. The Sahara is not the only obstacle to contact with the outside world. Africa's coastline is unbroken by bays, gulfs or inland seas. The result is that its coastline is shorter than Europe's, though Africa is three times the size of Europe. As it lacked anything like the Baltic, Mediterranean, or Black Sea, which open up the interior of Europe, Africa remained closed to most people from outside.

Africa is like an upside-down saucer. It is a vast plateau that falls away to the narrow coastal plain which surrounds the continent. Except for the Niger and the Zambezi, the great rivers of Africa plunge in falls and rapids from the plateau to the lowlands. This means that few rivers are navigable far inland.

The Songhai Empire

In the Middle Ages huge African empires had grown up as a result of trade across the Sahara. The greatest were Ghana and Mali. By 1500 these had declined and been replaced by Songhai. The Songhai people lived on the river Niger around the city of Gao. By the time of Askia the Great, who ruled from 1493 to 1528, the Songhai empire included great trading cities like Jenne and Timbuktu, which were also centres of Muslim learning. The empire controlled the main trade routes from West Africa to Tunis, Tripoli and Egypt. It remained important until the Moroccans sacked Timbuktu in 1593; their firearms were too much for the bowmen and cavalry of Songhai. This broke the power of Songhai. The main stream of West African trade now moved east to the Hausa states and Kano. By 1750 Islam was important here too.

This carving from West Africa shows Portuguese soldiers and a miniature ship's crow's nest or lookout point.

Since the 12th century Europeans had been wondering about Prester John, a Christian king and priest who, they believed, ruled in Africa beyond the lands controlled by Arabs. The Portuguese hoped that they would be able to reach Prester John's successor. In 1493 a Portuguese disguised as an Arab reached the court of the Christian emperor of Ethiopia – perhaps the king they were looking for – but alliance with him did not give them power in the African interior. This detail from a 16th-century Portuguese map (right) shows the legendary Prester John surveying his kingdom.

THE CONGO KINGDOM

Powerful kingdoms were rising in other parts of Africa too, among them the Luba and Lunda kingdoms in Central Africa and the Monomatapa in the Zambezi valley. When the Portuguese landed near the Congo river in 1484 they found a Congo kingdom there. In 1506 a Congolese Christian prince seized the throne with the help of the Portuguese, but there were never enough missionaries to convert his people. The Portuguese were more concerned with the slave trade than religion and by 1650 were openly at war with the Congolese. After the Portuguese victory the Congo state began to decline.

Europeans in Africa

The first Europeans in Africa were the Portuguese. They explored the coast when looking for a route to the Spice Islands and in 1482 they built the first of their forts on the Gold Coast. As they sailed up he coast of East Africa they reached Muslim ports which had been trade centres for 150 years. Through Sofala, for example, passed the gold trade of Mozambique and Zimbabwe. There were other thriving ports such as Kilwa and Mombasa, many of which the Portuguese captured or destroyed.

The Dutch followed the Portuguese and pushed them out of the Gold Coast by 1642, though the Portuguese continued to trade from their base at Luanda in Angola. It was a Dutchman, Jan van Riebeeck, who was sent by the Dutch East India Company to found a supply station at the Cape of Good Hope. Here Dutch ships on their way to India could stock up with fresh food and vegetables. Some Dutch settlers went inland, and started to farm. But most Europeans in Africa stayed on or near the coast. This was partly because it was difficult to travel inland, and partly because of deadly diseases such as malaria and yellow fever which thrived there. The main reason the Europeans stayed on the coast was that they had no need to go inland. Their chief interest was in slaves and these were brought to the coast by powerful African kingdoms such as Ashanti and Dahomey.

In 1750 Europeans controlled only small areas of Africa. The sources and courses of the great African rivers were unknown to them but in 1778 Sir Joseph Banks founded the Africa Association. This began to organize explorations and led to the opening up of Africa in the 19th century.

CHRONOLOGY

1482 First Portuguese fort on Gold Coast
1493 Askia the Great rules the Songhai empire
1498 Vasco da Gama sails round Africa to India
1505 Portuguese capture Kilwa
1506 Nzinga Mvemba becomes Christian king of the Congo
1513 Start of the slave trade across the Atlantic
1571 Portuguese begin conquest of Angola
1591 Moroccan invasion of Songhai empire
1593 Moroccans sack Timbuktu
1652 Jan van Riebeeck lands at the Cape of Good Hope
1665 Portuguese defeat Congolese army at the battle of Ambuila. Decline of Congo kingdom
1750 Ashanti empire conquers African states on Gold Coast

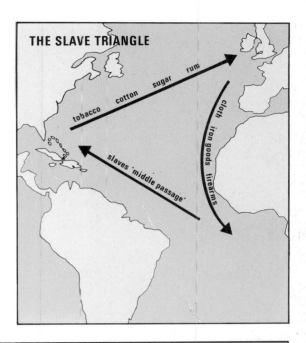

THE SLAVE TRIANGLE

THE SLAVE TRADE

Arabs had been trading in slaves on the East African coast before Europeans sailed round Africa, but it was Europeans who began this brutal trade on a huge scale. The Portuguese were the first to deal in slaves, but the British, Dutch and French soon joined in, so that over 10 million Africans were transported to America and the West Indies. There they produced cotton, sugar, rum and rice, which were exported to Europe. Guns, cloth and tools were sent to Africa to pay for the slaves and complete this triangular trade. The normal passage across the Atlantic lasted seven to eight weeks, during which many slaves died because of the overcrowded and filthy conditions on board. The description below is by Olaudah Equiano, a Nigerian who was captured by African slave dealers at the age of 11:

The stench of the hold was intolerably loathsome. The closeness of the place and the heat of the climate, added to the number in the ship, which was so crowded that each had scarcely room to turn himself, almost suffocated us. The air became unfit to breathe and many of the slaves fell sick and died. Our wretched situation was aggravated by the heavy chains on our legs, the filth of the necessary tubs, and the shrieks of women and the groans of the dying.

TIMBUKTU

A description by Leo Africanus, a Moor from Spain, who visited Songhai early in the 16th century:

The rich King of Timbuktu has many plates and sceptres of gold . . . and he keeps a magnificent court . . . He has always three thousand horsemen and a great many footmen, who shoot poisoned arrows, waiting upon him. They often have skirmishes with those who refuse to pay tribute and those they capture they sell [as slaves] to the merchants of Timbuktu . . . Here are many doctors, judges, priests and other learned men, who are well kept at the King's expense. And here are brought different manuscripts or written books out of Barbarie [North Africa], which are sold for more money than any other merchandise.

Willem Adriaan van der Stel, governor of Cape Colony from 1699 to 1707, on his farm. He is said to have made the first good South African wine.

45

Warfare

In the Middle Ages, wars were fought by mounted knights in heavy suits of armour, armed with lances and swords. Foot soldiers were chiefly archers and pikemen. The siege was an important part of warfare, and the siege machines used to attack heavily fortified castles were little different from those of ancient times. Towards the end of the period, however, the first firearms came into use. As they developed, so methods of warfare changed.

The First Hand Guns

Throughout the 16th century the Spaniards were the military leaders of Europe, as they were the first to make wide use of firearms. The arquebus, an early portable gun, revolutionized warfare. Gonzalo de Cordoba of Spain used arquebuses instead of crossbows. His victory over the French at Cerignola in 1503 made infantry carrying firearms the most important soldiers on the battlefield.

Hand guns were cheaper to make and easier to use than the crossbow. Later in the 16th century the matchlock musket gradually took over from the arquebus. It was heavy and needed a forked rest to support the barrel, and it could fire only one shot every two minutes, compared with the arquebus's one shot every minute. Its advantages were its greater range and reliability. It could crash through the heaviest armour at 275 metres (300 yards) and so it was most valuable against cavalry. Once they had fired, musketeers moved back into the protection of squares of pikemen, who did the real fighting. They checked the cavalry charge with their 5-metre (16-foot) long pikes, pulled riders off their horses with the hooks of their halberds and finished them off with their swords. By 1600 there was one musketeer in the Spanish armies for every pikeman and half of them had matchlocks.

Artillery and Siege Warfare

Improvements in artillery were just as important as changes in firearms. Great guns could knock down the walls of the strongest medieval castles, as Mehmet the Conqueror showed when he destroyed the walls of Constantinople in 1453.

As a result a new type of fortification had to be developed and warfare became more defensive. Fortifications were sunk deep into the ground, and instead of high walls there were low and very thick earth banks, sometimes faced with stone. Circular towers were replaced by four-sided angular works called bastions, which overlooked all possible approaches. Sieges were great set-pieces and replaced the open battle for a hundred years. There was no major battle in Europe between Mühlberg in 1534 and Breitenfeld in 1631.

Heavy artillery was useful only in sieges, as it was difficult to move and very expensive. In 1600 one gun needed 20 to 30 horses to pull it, and another 40 horses for the ammunition carts. One of the most successful people at siege warfare was Marshal Vauban in the reign of Louis XIV. He built 33 fortresses and improved 300 others on the borders of France, and carried out 55 successful sieges.

'The Lion of the North'

In the 17th century a new military power, Sweden, arose, led by Gustavus Adolphus. His reforms affected every part of 17th-century armies and were copied all over Europe. He supplied his infantry with a

These drawings show some items of a Swedish soldier's equipment, including a scythe, a cooking pot and a knapsack. They date from about 1700.

lighter musket, the wheellock, and introduced paper cartridges containing powder and shot, which made reloading quicker. His army still used pikes in attack (each squadron had 192 musketeers, but 216 pikemen) although he cut them down to a length of 2·5 metres (8 feet). His reform of artillery was even more important. He reduced the types of gun to three: 24-pounders for sieges, 12-pounders and 3-pounders. The last were light enough to be moved by one horse or three men. For the first time cannon could keep up with infantry on the battlefield. The 3-pounder had pre-packed rounds and a rate of fire slightly better than that of a musket.

Other countries sent their young officers to serve with and learn from the Swedes. The French copied them so successfully that from the 1640s to the 1690s they were the main military power in Europe. Oliver Cromwell's New Model Army also followed the Swedish example.

Flintlock Musket and Ring Bayonet
Two developments at the end of the 17th century were the flintlock musket and the ring bayonet. The matchlock, with its exposed gunpowder and lighted matches, was unsafe to load. The flint made a spark only when it was needed and was much safer. The plug bayonet had fitted into the muzzle of the musket and made firing impossible when it was fixed. The use of the ring bayonet, fastened to the outside of the barrel, meant that an infantryman could defend himself immediately after firing. The British Duke of Marlborough was one of the first generals to use both the flintlock musket (his 'Brown Bess') and the ring bayonet.

The pike was no longer needed and had almost disappeared by 1700. Infantry now formed in lines of three to six men deep and would stand in a hollow square when facing a cavalry charge. Cavalry remained important. The French used it mainly for its firepower, as the riders used pistols. Marlborough and the Austrian general

Suleyman the Magnificent was ruler of the Ottoman empire from 1520 to 1566. He greatly extended Ottoman power in eastern Europe and the Mediterranean. Here he is seen during his campaign to capture the island of Rhodes from the Knights Hospitallers. Under Suleyman the Ottomans had 30,000 soldiers; most of them were cavalry, carrying bows, lances and swords, but they also used artillery and muskets.

Prince Eugene, like Gustavus Adolphus, used a cavalry charge with drawn swords as shock tactics to decide a battle. All Marlborough's victories were completed in this way.

Frederick the Great
The last great general in this period was Frederick the Great of Prussia. He showed his brilliance in the Seven Years War (1756–1763), when Swedish, French, Russian, Austrian and some German armies were fighting against him. He managed to survive, a remarkable feat, by defeating each of his enemies in turn in a rapid war of movement. He believed in going on to the offensive rather than waiting to be attacked. His drill and discipline were severe – 'The men must fear their officers more than the enemy', he said – but, like Gustavus Adolphus, he was widely copied.

A British grenadier, from a tapestry showing the battle of Blenheim. Grenadiers, first used in about 1670, carried hand grenades as well as muskets. At first companies of grenadiers were attached to infantry regiments, from the 1750s on, they formed their own regiments.

Frederick the Great was nicknamed the 'Soldier King'. His army was a very efficient fighting machine. He introduced light, horsedrawn guns which could be moved from place to place during the course of a battle.

Great Voyages

In the 15th and 16th centuries Europeans attempting to reach Asia by sea find a new continent and the shape of those already known. The Portuguese become the first to sail round Africa to Asia when Vasco da Gama reaches India in 1498. The Spaniards try a western route but Columbus finds a new continent, America, in the way. Efforts are made to find a way round or through this continent; Magellan succeeds; and the English and Dutch, sailing northwards, fail but learn much about Canada and the Arctic. The Pacific remains largely unexplored until the 17th century. With Cook's explorations in the 18th century the voyages of discovery come to an end: the size and shape of all the continents are now accurately known.

John Cabot, born like Columbus in Genoa, looks for a North-West Passage to Asia on behalf of England. He reaches North America in 1497. Further attempts to find this Passage, led by **Frobisher**, **Baffin** and **Hudson**, fail as ice blocks the way, but they learn much about the North American coast.

Jacques Cartier for France tries to find a strait through North America and discovers the St Lawrence River (1535).

Henry Hudson, in Dutch service, sails up the Hudson River in 1609.

Magellan, looking for a way round South America, discovers the straits named after him, crosses the Pacific and is killed in the Philippines (1521). **Del Cano** continues, reaches Spain and becomes the first to sail round the world.

Christopher Columbus discovers the West Indies, which he thinks are part of Asia, and the coast of Central America and Venezuela (1492–1504).

Amerigo Vespucci explores the coast of South America, which he is the first to call *Mundus Novus* (New World), from 1497. Martin Waldseemüller, a map-maker, in 1507 calls this New World 'America' after Vespucci, who used the Latin name Americus Vespucius.

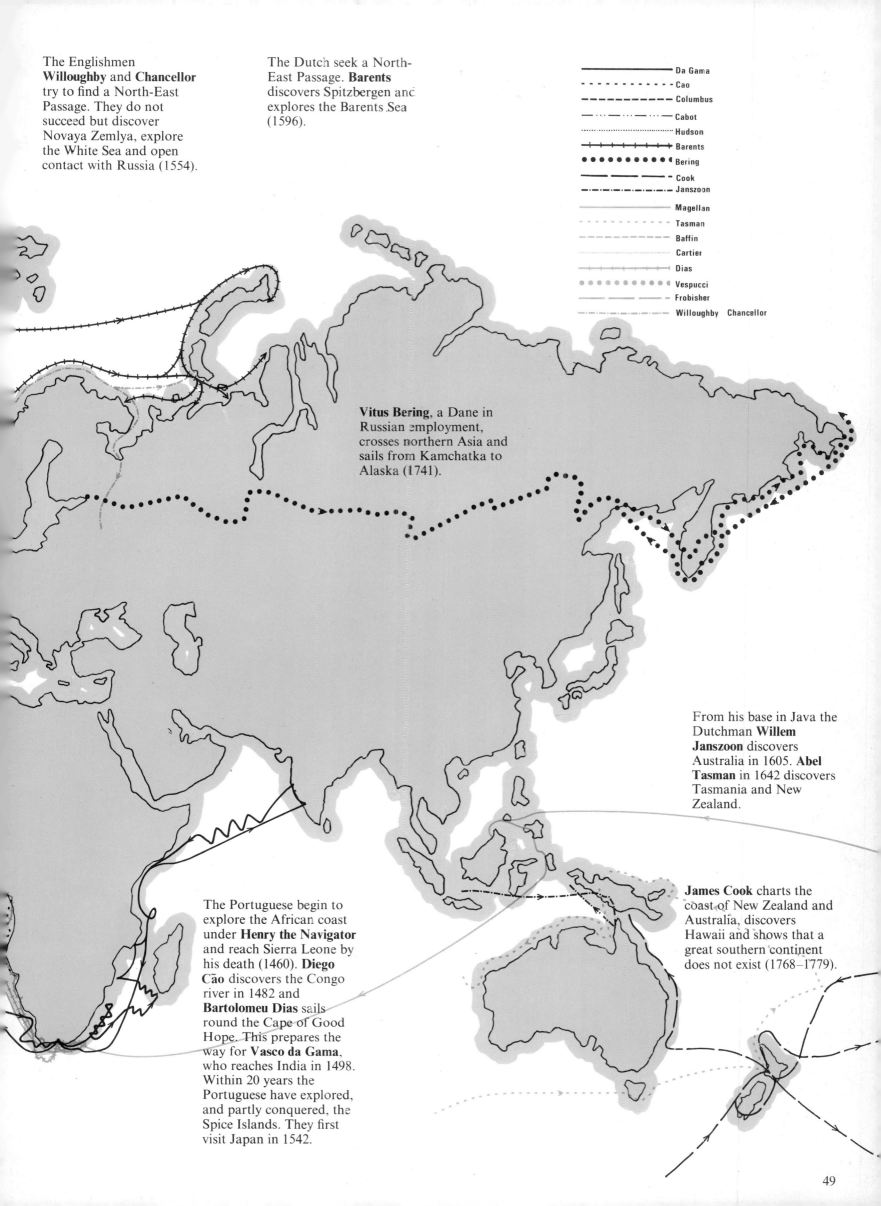

The Englishmen **Willoughby** and **Chancellor** try to find a North-East Passage. They do not succeed but discover Novaya Zemlya, explore the White Sea and open contact with Russia (1554).

The Dutch seek a North-East Passage. **Barents** discovers Spitzbergen and explores the Barents Sea (1596).

Vitus Bering, a Dane in Russian employment, crosses northern Asia and sails from Kamchatka to Alaska (1741).

From his base in Java the Dutchman **Willem Janszoon** discovers Australia in 1605. **Abel Tasman** in 1642 discovers Tasmania and New Zealand.

The Portuguese begin to explore the African coast under **Henry the Navigator** and reach Sierra Leone by his death (1460). **Diego Cão** discovers the Congo river in 1482 and **Bartolomeu Dias** sails round the Cape of Good Hope. This prepares the way for **Vasco da Gama**, who reaches India in 1498. Within 20 years the Portuguese have explored, and partly conquered, the Spice Islands. They first visit Japan in 1542.

James Cook charts the coast of New Zealand and Australia, discovers Hawaii and shows that a great southern continent does not exist (1768–1779).

————————	Da Gama
–·–·–·–·–·	Cao
– – – – – –	Columbus
—·—·—·—	Cabot
·············	Hudson
+++++++	Barents
●●●●●●●	Bering
– – – – –	Cook
—··—··—	Janszoon
————————	Magellan
·············	Tasman
– – – – – –	Baffin
·············	Cartier
+++++++	Dias
●●●●●●●	Vespucci
– – – – –	Frobisher
—··—··—	Willoughby Chancellor

India

The Portuguese were the first Europeans to set up bases on the coast of India. When Vasco da Gama reached India he said that he had come to look for 'Christians and Spices' and he made no attempt to seize territory. It was Albuquerque who captured Goa in 1510. This was followed by the capture of other ports. But the Portuguese never tried any large-scale conquest in India.

When the Dutch were at war with Spain and Portugal in 1580, they could no longer pick up spices in Lisbon or Cadiz, so they decided to take them directly from the East Indies. They first sent a fleet to the East in 1595, and in 1602 they formed their East India Company. They built trading stations on the coast of India and captured Ceylon (Sri Lanka), where they could buy pepper and cinnamon, from the Portuguese. But India was less important to them than the Spice Islands. The two countries to which India was really important were England and France.

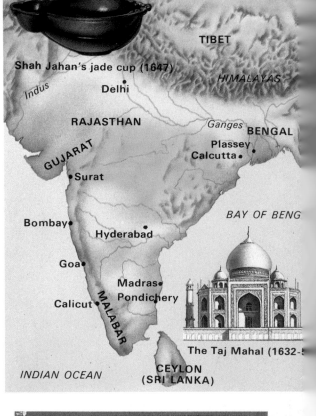

The port of Calicut, on the Malabar coast of southern India, was a busy Arab trading centre when Vasco da Gama reached it in 1498. It was a Portuguese trading post for a short time, and then the English East India Company set up a base there. It was famous for its cotton cloth and gave its name to the Indian cotton cloth known as calico.

The English East India Company

The English founded an East India Company shortly before the Dutch. They began to trade with the Spice Islands, but were driven out by the Dutch. This led the English to concentrate on India. They gained control of the sea by defeating a Portuguese fleet off Surat, and the Mughal emperor gave them permission to trade in return for their fleet's protection of Muslim pilgrims on their way to the holy city of Mecca.

By 1700 the English had set up more trading stations in India: at Madras in the south, Bombay in the west (this became English when a Portuguese princess married Charles II in 1662) and Calcutta in the east. Trade was mainly in cotton goods, indigo from Gujarat, pepper from the Malabar coast, silks and saltpetre (used for making gunpowder) from Bengal. In return the Indians bought lead and tin but many Indian goods had to be paid for in silver. The English, like the Portuguese and the Dutch, also carried goods between one part of Asia and another. Some ships were sent from India to China for tea, which by 1700 had become the national drink in England.

Right: A painting of a Frenchman from Rajasthan in north-west India, around, 1700. Below: The Mughal Emperor Aurangzeb is given the head of his brother, whom he had killed as a rival for the throne. Aurangzeb's ruthless rule hastened the break-up of the Mughal empire.

The French in India

The French too began to trade in India after the formation of their East India Company in 1664. They established two major trading posts, at Chandernagore near Calcutta and Pondichéry near Madras. In the 17th century Europeans could trade in India because the Mughal emperors allowed them to do so. The emperors could have driven the English or the French out, if they had wanted to. The situation changed with the collapse of the Mughal empire after the death of Aurangzeb in 1707. After that Indian governors in the provinces paid little attention to the emperor in Delhi and behaved like independent rulers. They had to be wooed by the Europeans.

The directors of the English and French East India Companies were concerned only with profit and not with conquest but it took a year to send messages to India, so many company officials acted without waiting for instructions from London or Paris. The first European to interfere in Indian affairs on a large scale was the French governor Dupleix. As he had few French troops he trained Indian soldiers (*sepoys*) in the same way as he trained the French. These enabled him to back up various Indian princes.

When Britain and France were at war in Europe, they also fought in India. In 1746 the French captured Madras but they had to give it up when peace was made in 1748, in exchange for Cape Breton Island, which the British had captured in North America.

Dupleix was recalled to France in 1754 but he left the French in a stronger position in India than the British, and with more Indian allies when war broke out again two years later. This, the Seven Years War (see page 41), was to be a turning-point in the

history of India, just as it was in North America. Control of the sea and the leadership of Robert Clive turned the tide in favour of the British, who could take troops and supplies out from England while preventing the French from receiving reinforcements. After the defeat of the Indian army of Siraj-ud daula at Plassey, Clive took control of the rich area of Bengal. The end came in 1760 with the defeat of the French at Wandiwash and the fall of their base at Pondichéry.

When peace was made in 1763 the French kept their trading stations in India but they were not to be fortified. The French were allowed to stay only as traders. Clive's victory meant that the British in India were to take the place of the Mughals. India was the base which, in the 19th century, enabled Britain to expand into the rest of South Asia and into the Far East as well.

CHRONOLOGY
1510 Albuquerque captures Goa for Portugal
1600 English East India Company formed
1618 Mughal emperor gives English the right to trade at Surat
1623 The Amboina 'massacre': the Dutch finally push the English out of the Spice Islands
1658 Dutch take Ceylon from the Portuguese
1662 England gets Bombay when Charles II marries Catherine of Braganza
1664 French East India Company formed
1707 Death of the last great Mughal emperor
1742 Dupleix becomes governor of the French settlements in India
1746 The French capture Madras
1748 Madras restored to Britain in exchange for Cape Breton Island
1754 Dupleix recalled to France
1757 Battle of Plassey – Clive defeats Siraj-ud daula and takes control of Bengal
1760 French defeat at Wandiwash
1763 Peace of Paris leaves Britain dominant in India

The Mughal Emperor Shah Alam hands Robert Clive of the East India Company documents which grant him the right to collect revenues.

The Scientific Revolution

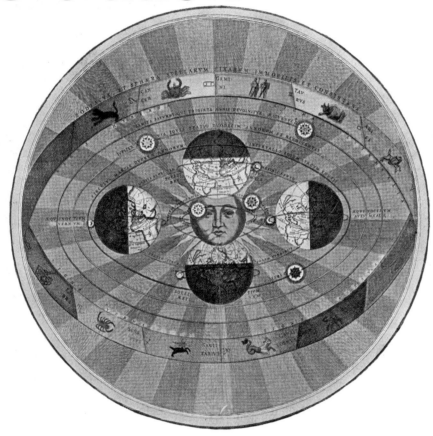

In the Middle Ages people in western Europe considered life on Earth of little importance compared with eternal life in Heaven. The most important knowledge was what the Church taught. This was that the universe had been created to serve people's needs and that the Earth was at the centre of the universe. The Sun and planets moved in circles round the Earth. In the 16th century these ideas were challenged, and a Scientific Revolution began which was to lead to new understanding of the way in which things work.

The Revolution in Astronomy
The first person to challenge the established ideas seriously was Nicolaus Copernicus. In 1543 he put forward the theory that the Earth and planets moved round the Sun and that the Earth rotates daily on its axis. To most people this seemed against common sense: if the Earth revolved, would not its movement create a mighty wind? Copernicus did not bring about a scientific revolution, as not for another 150 years was there a satisfactory way of explaining why the Earth and the planets behaved as Copernicus said they did.

Some evidence to support Copernicus was provided by Galileo Galilei. He built his own telescope and discovered the moons of Jupiter, which revolved round the planet.

The Solar System, as described by the Polish scientist Nicolaus Copernicus in 1543, showing the Sun and not the Earth at the centre of the Universe. Copernicus was educated first at Cracow in Poland and later went to the great Italian universities at Padua, Bologna and Ferrara.

Vesalius with one of his anatomical models. He was born in Brussels in 1514 and published the first complete description of human anatomy in 1543. His works, which were beautifully and clearly illustrated, were based on the anatomy he learned by dissecting dead bodies. This led him into serious trouble with the Church authorities.

This showed that the Earth was not the only centre of movement in the sky. Galileo became an enthusiastic supporter of Copernicus's ideas and for this he was brought before the Inquisition (the Church's council to inquire into possible heresy) in 1633. In 1600 the Inquisition had burned Giordano Bruno at the stake for saying the Earth moved round the Sun, as this was against the teaching of the Church. Galileo had to withdraw his views.

There was no satisfactory explanation of Copernicus's view until the work of Isaac Newton, who was born in 1642, the

A microscope used by the English physicist Robert Hooke in the late 17th century. In his work 'Micrographia' he described the plant and animal cells he had seen through the microscope. This led to its wider use. He also studied the movement of light and of stars and planets, assisted Newton, invented the wheel barometer and began to use spiral springs in watch balances. From 1677 to 1683 he was secretary to the Royal Society in London.

In 1752 the American Benjamin Franklin showed the electrical nature of lightning by flying a kite in a thunderstorm and drawing sparks from a key tied to the lower end of its string.

year of Galileo's death. Galileo had already put forward the idea that a body continues in motion in a straight line until something stops or deflects it. Newton accepted this; but if it was true why did the Earth not move in a straight line away from the Sun? One of Newton's friends told how the great scientist thought of an answer to this question when he saw an apple falling from a tree: the same gravity which pulled the apple towards the Earth, prevented the Earth from leaving the Sun and the Moon from leaving the Earth. In his *Mathematical Principles* of 1687 Newton showed mathematically how the force of gravity worked.

Medicine

The Scientific Revolution was not limited to astronomy, physics and mathematics. In 1543, the same year in which Copernicus published his book, Vesalius's *The Fabric of the Human Body* appeared. It had detailed illustrations and was the result of Vesalius's dissections of human bodies. Vesalius showed the structure of the human body and so prepared the way for others, who would show how it worked.

One of these was William Harvey, who studied at Padua in Italy where Vesalius and Galileo had been professors. Harvey found by careful experiment that the amount of blood the heart would throw out in an hour was greater than the weight of a person. It was impossible to say where it went unless it circulated round the body. He also showed that valves in the veins would allow blood to flow only towards the heart, while valves in the arteries permitted blood to flow away from the heart. His book, published in 1628, did not give a complete account of the circulation of the blood, as he did not know how the blood got from the arteries to the veins. The final proof of Harvey's teaching came in 1661, when capillaries (tubes connecting the arteries and veins) were discovered by using a microscope. All modern physiology has been based on Harvey's work.

The Spread of Scientific Knowledge

In the Middle Ages books had to be copied out by hand, a very slow and expensive process. Ideas therefore did not spread quickly. With the invention of the printing press books became cheaper and more easily available. Learned men could now get their works into the hands of colleagues in a few months.

The rise of scientific societies also helped the spread of ideas. Academies were first formed in Italy; in England the Royal Society (so called because Charles II was a member) was established in 1662, and in 1666 the Academy of Sciences was founded in Paris by Louis XIV. These societies collected facts, carried out experiments and published journals, so that others could learn about the latest ideas and discoveries.

The Scientific Revolution was important because it taught people that they must not rely on what the Greeks or Arabs had written in the past, but they must make their own observations. They must question everything and test their theories by experiment to see if they were true. It was this critical attitude which made possible the great scientific and industrial advances of the 19th and 20th centuries, which were to affect the whole world so deeply.

Discovering the Pacific

In the Middle Ages people believed that there was a great southern continent, which they called Terra Australis or South Land. By the 16th century geographers had decided that it must lie in the South Pacific, somewhere between Africa and Cape Horn, the southernmost tip of South America.

The Dutch Discover Australia

The Spaniards seemed well placed to explore the Pacific, as they had bases in Mexico and Peru and traded between Acapulco in Mexico and the Philippines. Unfortunately the south-east trade winds pushed ships north towards the Equator and made it almost impossible for ships from Mexico to enter the south Pacific. Exploration of this area would have to start from the west, around the Cape of Good Hope, from where ships could sail with the westerly winds. The first to do this were the Dutch, who sailed from the Cape to Java. In 1605 Willem Janszoon left Java to survey the southern coast of New Guinea. He became the first European to discover Australia, which the Dutch called New Holland. By 1642 the Dutch had explored the whole of the west coast and part of the north and south coast of Australia.

In that year Abel Tasman sailed from Batavia, heading first south and then east. He discovered the island later named Tasmania after him, and journeyed on till he reached New Zealand, which he thought was part of Terra Australis. He then returned to the Dutch East Indies by sailing north and west, and so proved that Australia was an island.

James Cook

After Tasman's voyage there was little interest in a southern continent until the British Admiralty sent Samuel Wallis and Philip Carteret to discover it in 1766. Instead Wallis rediscovered Tahiti, though he was certain 'we saw the long wished for Southern Continent'.

Another expedition was sent in 1768. It was led by Captain James Cook who had joined the British navy as a seaman in 1755. He was a skilful navigator and surveyor and helped to chart the St Lawrence river before the British attack on Quebec in 1759. Cook was very popular with his crew and much concerned about their health. He was horrified that so many men on a long voyage died from scurvy. To prevent this he insisted that his men ate sauerkraut (a kind of pickled cabbage), fruit and carrots.

A drawing by Abel Tasman showing native boats, Dutch ships, and Fiji islanders.

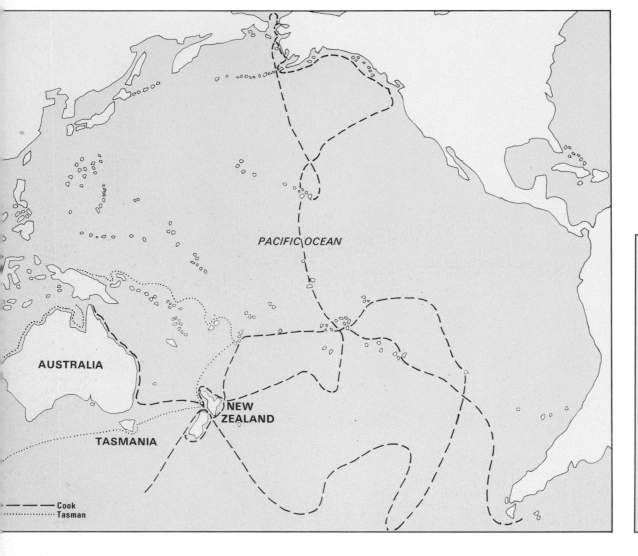

PACIFIC OCEAN

AUSTRALIA

NEW ZEALAND

TASMANIA

– – – – Cook
·········· Tasman

Cook's First and Second Voyages

Astronomers forecast that in 1769 the planet Venus would move across the face of the Sun, something that would not happen again for another hundred years. Cook was sent to the Pacific to observe this and reached Tahiti by sailing round Cape Horn. He next sailed to New Zealand, found the strait between North and South Islands and charted nearly 4000 kilometres (2400 miles) of coast. He claimed New Zealand for Britain before sailing on to the unknown east coast of Australia. He kept close to the shore so that he could chart the coast, only to find that the Great Barrier Reef lay between his ship *The Endeavour* and the sea. His ship was holed and only managed to reach the open sea with great difficulty. Cook charted 3200 kilometres (2000 miles) of the Australian coast, claimed it for Britain and returned home in 1771.

Cook was soon off on his second voyage to the Pacific, this time by sailing round the Cape of Good Hope. He was instructed to sail round the Earth in as southerly a latitude as possible. This he did. Keeping close to 60° he crossed the Antarctic Circle three times, the first man to do so. This too was full of dangers. There was dense fog and towering icebergs threatened to destroy his two small ships, but he proved without any doubt that the fabled southern continent stretching right across the world did not exist.

Death in Hawaii

Cook set sail on his last voyage to the Pacific in 1776. He was looking for a north-west passage linking the Atlantic and Pacific Oceans. He charted the North American Pacific coastline, and sailed through the Bering Strait separating America from Asia, before ice blocked his progress. Cook then turned back for Hawaii, which he had discovered earlier. The natives tired of the Englishmen demanding food from them. There was a quarrel, in which Cook was stabbed to death and cut into pieces.

THE DEATH OF COOK
James King, one of Cook's lieutenants, describes his death:

An accident happened which gave a fatal turn. The boats, having fired at some canoes, killed a chief. The [islanders] armed themselves and a general attack followed. Our unfortunate Commander was stabbed in the back, and fell with his face in the water. His body was immediately dragged ashore and surrounded by the enemy, who . . . showed a savage eagerness to share in his destruction. Thus fell our great and excellent Commander!

This drawing of red honeysuckle was made by Sydney Parkinson on one of Cook's voyages. Before the days of photography, drawings were an important record of explorers' finds.

This picture of Cook's ships 'Resolution' and 'Adventure' at Tahit was painted by William Hodges, who travelled with him.

Captain Cook. His detailed surveys and observations set new standards for the explorers who followed him.

FROM CAPTAIN COOK'S JOURNALS
Australia, June 11–12, 1770:

A few Minutes before 11 the Ship Struck. We found that we had got upon a reef of Coral. The ship being quite fast we throw'd over board our guns, Iron and stone ballast, Casks, Hoops, staves, oyle Jars, decay'd stores etc. About 20 past 10 o'Clock the Ship floated, we having at this time 3 feet 9 inches water in the hold . . . At 8 hauld her bow close a shore which gave us an opportunity to examine the leak. The whole was cut away as if by a blunt edge tool. A large piece of Coral rock was sticking in one hole and several pieces of fothering [caulking], small stones, sand etc. had stoped the water.

Tahiti, September 1, 1777:

A man was to be sacrificed. The unhappy victim seemed to be a middle-aged man; and one of the lowest class of the people. They generally make choice of guilty persons or else of common, low, fellows, who stroll about without any fixed abode. We were told that he had been knocked on the head with a stone. Those who are [selected] to suffer are never apprized of their fate, till the blow is given.

Domingo (now Haiti). In 1750 over one sixth of France's foreign trade was in sugar. The West Indies and the north coast of Brazil provided Europe with most of its coffee, rice and cotton, as well as sugar. They were looked upon as Europe's most valuable overseas possessions.

The North American colonies were populated largely by Europeans: English, French and Dutch. They produced grain, meat and butter, except for plantations in the south where tobacco and rice were grown. As the northern colonies could not sell their produce in Europe (the voyage was too long for perishable foods), they found a market in the West Indies, which concentrated on crops for export. The money they received meant that American farmers could buy Scottish linen, hardware from Birmingham and all sorts of other English manufactured goods.

Trade with Asia

European trade with Asia was not as great as with America, because there was no demand for European goods in Asia. In 1793 the Chinese Emperor Ch'ien Lung told King George III: 'As your Ambassador can see for himself, we possess all things. I set no value on objects strange or ingenious and have no use for your country's manufactures.' Cotton goods from India were popular in Europe, as they were colourful, cheap and washable, though there

World Trade in 1763

By 1750 a large, world-wide network of trade had developed for the first time. The main articles of trade were gold and silver from Spanish America, cotton goods from India, tea and silk from China, spices from the East Indies, sugar from the West Indies and Brazil and slaves from Africa. The centre of this trade was western Europe, as it was countries there which made the discoveries and whose well-armed ships controlled the trade routes.

Transatlantic Trade

Europe traded more with America than with Asia. The main reason was the great demand in Europe for West Indian sugar. Sugar had long been known in Asia and small amounts had reached Europe, where they were sold at very high prices. About 1640 sugar was introduced into the West Indies and from the start was very profitable. A Barbados plantation that had been sold for £400 in 1640 was worth £14,000 by 1648. The countries that benefitted most from this trade were England and France, who owned the richest sugar island, San

A Dutch merchant ship of the late 17th century battles through a storm. In 1760 Holland still carried more trade goods than any other nation.

PLANTS AND ANIMALS

One effect of international trade was the spread of plants and animals from one continent to another, something which greatly increased the world's food supply. Horses, cattle and sheep, which had been unknown in America, were brought there from Europe, as were cereals like wheat, rye, oats and barley. All these thrived in their new country. Spaniards took the olive, vine and a variety of fruits to their empire in America. From America to Europe and Africa went maize, potatoes, tomatoes and peanuts. Cacao, from which the Aztecs and Mayas made *chocolatl* also came from America.

In addition to food, American Indians grew two crops which were soon produced on a large scale. These were tobacco and cotton. Tobacco was used by American Indians in all forms known today – in pipes, cigars, cigarettes rolled in corn husks and as snuff. From America tobacco rapidly spread all over the world. Cotton was known in many parts of the world before 1500 but the cotton used today largely comes from varieties originally produced by the American Indians.

were attempts by European governments to limit their import as they competed with European-made textiles.

Asian goods had to be paid for in gold or silver, most of which came from Spanish America. A complicated pattern of trade grew up which linked the American colonies with Europe, with each other and with Asia. The Frenchman Voltaire summed this up clearly in the second half of the 18th century:

People ask what becomes of all the gold and silver which is continually flowing into Spain from Peru and Mexico. It goes into the pockets of Frenchmen and Englishmen and Dutchmen, who carry on trade in Cadiz, and in return send the products of their industries to America. A large part of this money goes to the East Indies and pays for silk, spices, saltpetre, sugar-candy, tea, textiles, diamonds and curios.

The Spread of Peoples

Trade and the voyages of discovery also led to the movement of peoples from their place of origin to different parts of the world. In 1652 some Dutchmen settled in South Africa, where their descendants remain today, but the greatest change came in America. Much of the native population in America was killed off after the arrival of Europeans, either in fighting or, most often, because the Indians had no resistance to diseases brought from Europe. The disappearing Indians were replaced by European settlers and slaves from Africa. In South and Central America Spanish and Portuguese settlers often took Indian wives. As a result a *mestizo* (mixed) population grew up, which in some parts came to outnumber both Europeans and Indians.

On the Atlantic seaboard of America there were few Indians. Europeans settled here. They cleared the land, lived by their own labour and came to settle in increasing numbers right up to the 20th century. As a result, North America today is populated by people of European stock. A different type of settlement occurred in the West Indies, northern Brazil and the southern part of North America. Much labour was needed there for sugar and tobacco plantations, so slaves were brought from Africa and soon outnumbered the whites. Today the population of the West Indies is mainly Negro.

World trade developed enormously in the 18th century before there was an Industrial Revolution. Between 1702 and 1772 Britain's foreign trade trebled, while that of France almost caught it up. There was also a change in the direction of trade. In 1700 most of Britain's trade was with Europe; by 1770 two-thirds of it was outside Europe. It was owing to this increased trade abroad and the demand for British manufactures, particularly in America, that Britain was able to take the lead in the Industrial Revolution at the end of the 18th century.

Part of a silk-embroidered cotton hanging from western India, made towards the end of the 17th century. Textiles from India were taken to Europe in great quantities.

Left: Growing sugar on Martinique, in the West Indies, which was settled by the French in 1635. Sugar is still its chief industry.

Making sugar in 1749. Columbus took sugar cane with him on his second voyage to the West Indies and the Spaniards introduced it to Central and South America. By 1600 sugar production in the Americas was the largest industry in the world.

The World in 1763

In Europe 1763 sees the end of the Seven Years War and marks the rise of a new military power in the north, Prussia. Elsewhere the most important event is the triumph of Britain over France in America and India. Britain now dominates the seas and has the largest empire of any European country. The struggle for the Baltic has ended with the defeat of Sweden and the victory of Russia. Islam is on the defensive. The Ottoman Turks have lost some of their lands in Central Europe to the Habsburgs and have begun a long decline. Very different is the Chinese empire, which has never been as large as it is now.

6 Northern Europe Prussia under Frederick the Great is the new military power in Germany. It has taken Silesia where iron ore and coal are produced, and keeps it at the end of the Seven Years War. Russia has gained a foothold on the Baltic, where Peter the **7** Great has built his new capital, St Petersburg. Sweden has lost most of its lands on the southern shore of the Baltic.

Petit Trianon, Versailles, France

1 The Americas France ceases to have an empire in North America, giving up all its territories east of the Mississippi to Britain and those west of it to Spain. The Spaniards are pushing north from New Spain into **2** California.

Gravestone, Massachusetts

3 Western Europe Spain and its colonies are no longer ruled by the Habsburgs but by a Bourbon king. Spain's possessions in the Netherlands and Italy have passed to the Austrian **4** Habsburgs. France under Louis XIV has enlarged its frontiers in the north and east by taking Alsace, Lorraine, Franche Comté and part of the Spanish Netherlands. England has **5** united with Scotland in 1707 and together they are known as Britain.

8 Africa The Ashanti empire conquers African states on the Gold Coast and brings slaves to the coast for sale to Europeans. The Dutch have founded a **9** settlement at the Cape of Good Hope to provide Dutch ships on their way to the East with fresh food and vegetables. Dutch settlers are moving inland.

Part of a painting showing the many different peoples of the South Pacific region. It records the discoveries of Captain Cook and of the French explorer La Pérouse, who explored the Pacific from 1785 until his expedition was lost in the New Hebrides in 1788.

Church at Ouro Preto, Brazil

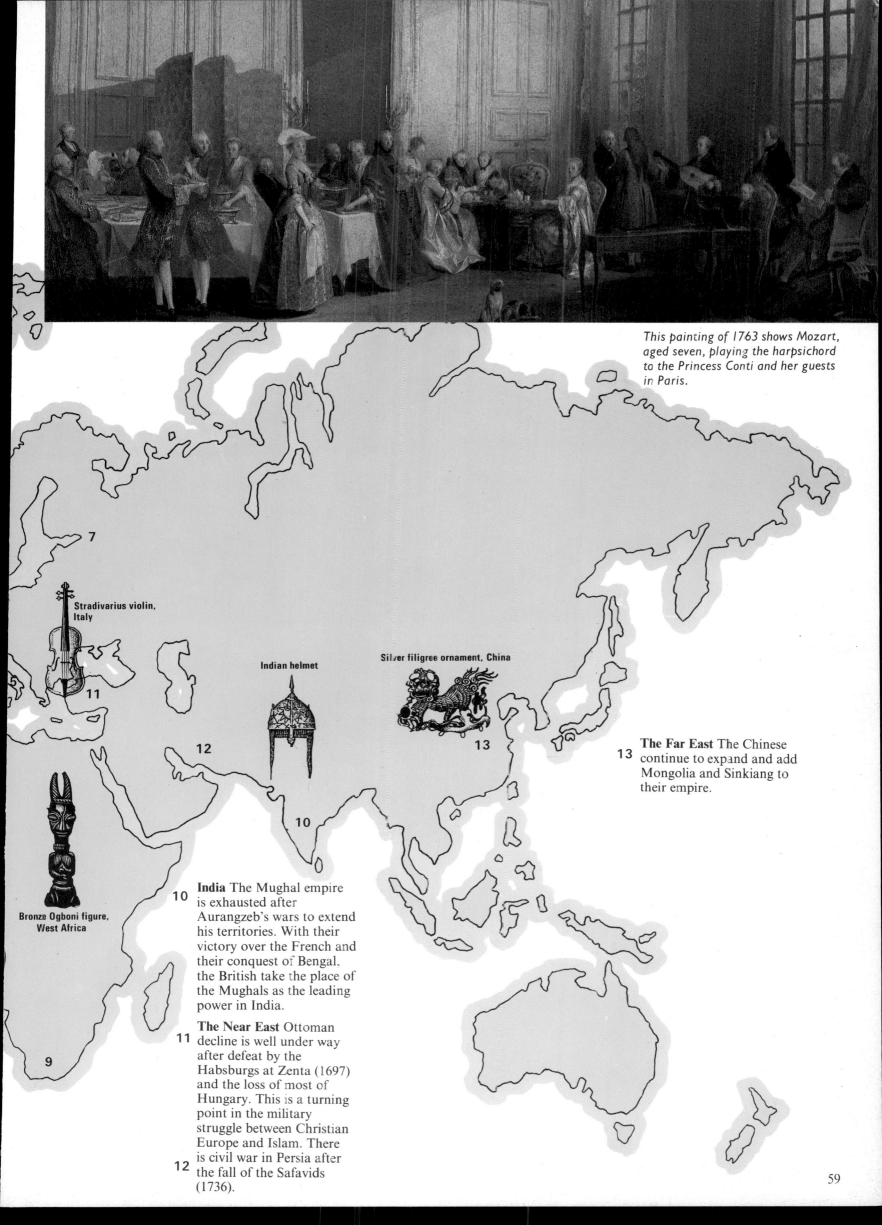

This painting of 1763 shows Mozart, aged seven, playing the harpsichord to the Princess Conti and her guests in Paris.

Stradivarius violin, Italy

Indian helmet

Silver filigree ornament, China

Bronze Ogboni figure, West Africa

The Far East The Chinese continue to expand and add Mongolia and Sinkiang to their empire.

India The Mughal empire is exhausted after Aurangzeb's wars to extend his territories. With their victory over the French and their conquest of Bengal, the British take the place of the Mughals as the leading power in India.

The Near East Ottoman decline is well under way after defeat by the Habsburgs at Zenta (1697) and the loss of most of Hungary. This is a turning point in the military struggle between Christian Europe and Islam. There is civil war in Persia after the fall of the Safavids (1736).

59

Index

Index

Glossary

Ally A state connected to another state by treaty or agreement.
Artillery Mounted firearms, such as cannon.
Astronomy The study of stars and planets to find out what they are made of and how they move.
Barbarians People living outside the frontiers of a dominant country.
Bullion Gold or silver in a mass, rather than in coins.
Caravan Group of merchants travelling together, usually for safety, through a desert or hostile region.
Catholic Church The Christian Church headed by the Pope in Rome.
Civilization A stage in society when people have highly developed skills and ways of living together.
Civil war War between groups of citizens of the same country.
Colonize To found settlements abroad.
Colony Group of people living in a new country, but keeping ties with their home country.
Conquistador The name, meaning 'conqueror' in Spanish, given to the Spanish adventurers who went to South America in search of treasure.
Cossacks Frontiersmen of southern Russia.
Counter-Reformation The movement within the Catholic Church to reform its practices.

Doctrine The teachings and beliefs officially held by a body such as the Church.
Dynasty A ruling family.
Expedition A journey taken for a special purpose.
Export To send goods outside the home country for sale abroad.
Feudal system A system of land ownership whereby a ruler or great lord owns the land and grants it to lesser lords or peasants in return for service.
Gravity The pull of a large body, such as the Earth, on smaller bodies.
Great Britain The name given to the kingdoms of England and Scotland after their Union in 1707.
Indulgence According to the Catholic Church, sins must be suffered for even if they have been forgiven. An indulgence takes away some of the suffering due for these sins.
Islam The religion which holds that Allah is the only God and Muhammad is his prophet. Islam also means the civilization built by followers of Muhammad.
Missionaries Those sent to make new converts to Christianity, particularly in foreign lands.
Monsoon Wind that blows at certain times of the year, particularly in the Indian Ocean and southern Asia.
Muslim Follower of Islam.
Navigation The art or practice of steering a particular course, and the skills that enable a course to be held.
Netherlands Until 1609, the name for the area which is now Belgium and the Kingdom of the Netherlands

(Holland). At that time the northern part, the United Provinces, or Holland, gained independence; the southern part (modern Belgium) was called the Spanish Netherlands.
Nomads People who move with their flocks and herds in search of grazing lands.
Plantation A large group of plants tended by workers living on the land under the direction of an authority.
Protestants Christians headed by Luther, who broke away from the Catholic Church, after trying to change practices to which they objected.
Reformation The movement headed by Luther to reform the Catholic Church. Luther particularly objected to the sale of indulgences by the Church.
Scurvy Disease of sailors on long sea-voyages. It was caused by the lack of ascorbic acid, found in fresh fruit and vegetables.
Sepoys Indian soldiers trained to serve with European armies.
Spice Islands Name given to the islands of South-East Asia from which spices were exported to Europe.
Steppes High, cold plains of Russia and Central Asia.
Tributaries Streams that feed a larger stream or lake.
Tsar Russian form of the word 'caesar', used for the ruler.
Tundra A treeless plain in the arctic region, with a subsoil that is permanently frozen.
Viceroy The governor of a country who rules as the representative of his king.

ACKNOWLEDGEMENTS
Photographs: cover National Gallery, London; endpapers British Museum; title page Science Museum, London; editorial bottom left: India Office Library, top right: Zefa; contents centre right: Michael Holford; page 8 National Gallery; page 9 top & bottom: Michael Holford; page 10 Science Museum, London; page 11 bottom: National Maritime Museum; page 13 bottom right: National Gallery of Art, Washington; page 15 top: National Maritime Museum; page 16 centre: British Museum; page 17 Michael Holford; page 19 top: Zefa, bottom: British Museum; page 20 Mansell; page 21 top: Scala, bottom: Mansell; page 22 Scala/Prado Madrid; page 23 top: Sonia Halliday Photos, bottom: National Maritime Museum; page 25 top: reproduced by Gracious Permission of Her Majesty The Queen, bottom: Victoria & Albert Museum, London; page 27 top: Victoria & Albert Museum, London, bottom: Sonia Halliday Photos/Jane Taylor; page 28 Allan Hutchison; page 29 top: British Museum, bottom: National Maritime Museum; page 30 top: Mansell; page 31 top: Victoria & Albert Museum, bottom: Mary Evans Picture Library; page 32 Michael Holford; page 33 top & bottom right: National Army Museum, bottom left: Mansell; page 34 Bodleian Library; page 35 centre: British Museum, bottom: Mary Evans Picture Library; page 36 Musées de la Ville de Strasburg; page 37 National Maritime Museum; page 39 top: Aldus Books, bottom: British Museum; page 40 Aldus Books; page 41 top: British Museum, bottom: Colour Library International; page 43 top Ian Hamilton; page 44 top left & bottom: British Museum; page 45 Mansell; page 46 top: Stetens Museum fur Kunst, Copenhagen, bottom: Kungl Armemuseum, Stockholm; page 47 top: Sonia Halliday Photos, bottom right: Mansell; page 50 top: British Museum, centre: British Museum, bottom: Mary Evans Picture Library; page 51 India Office Library; page 52 top: Ronan Picture Library, bottom: Science Museum; page 53 top: Science Museum, bottom left: Mansell; page 54 Mansell; page 55 centre: Michael Holford, bottom right: Michael Holford/National Maritime Museum, bottom left: National Maritime Museum; page 56 Victoria & Albert Museum; page 57 top: Victoria & Albert Museum, bottom left: Zefa, bottom right: Mansell; page 58 Michael Holford/Mrs Rienits; page 59 Scala/Louvre.
Picture Research: Penny Warn